The Unit Testing Practice Cookbook

Bulletproof Unit Testing with .NET

Anthony Giretti

Apress®

The Unit Testing Practice Cookbook: Bulletproof Unit Testing with .NET

Anthony Giretti
Montreal, QC, Canada

ISBN-13 (pbk): 979-8-8688-1453-2   ISBN-13 (electronic): 979-8-8688-1454-9
https://doi.org/10.1007/979-8-8688-1454-9

Copyright © 2025 by Anthony Giretti

Managing Director, Apress Media LLC: Welmoed Spahr
Acquisitions Editor: Ryan Byrnes
Coordinating Editor: Gryffin Winkler

Cover image designed by benzoix on freepik (www.freepik.com)

Distributed to the book trade worldwide by Springer Science+Business Media New York, 1 New York Plaza, New York, NY 10004. Phone 1-800-SPRINGER, fax (201) 348-4505, e-mail orders-ny@ springer-sbm.com, or visit www.springeronline.com. Apress Media, LLC is a Delaware LLC and the sole member (owner) is Springer Science + Business Media Finance Inc (SSBM Finance Inc). SSBM Finance Inc is a **Delaware** corporation.

For information on translations, please e-mail booktranslations@springernature.com; for reprint, paperback, or audio rights, please e-mail bookpermissions@springernature.com.

Apress titles may be purchased in bulk for academic, corporate, or promotional use. eBook versions and licenses are also available for most titles. For more information, reference our Print and eBook Bulk Sales web page at http://www.apress.com/bulk-sales.

Any source code or other supplementary material referenced by the author in this book can be found here: https://www.apress.com/gp/services/source-code.

If disposing of this product, please recycle the paper

Table of Contents

About the Author vii

About the Technical Reviewer ix

Acknowledgments xi

Introduction xiii

Chapter 1: Introducing Unit Testing Practice 1

Introduction to Testing Practice 1

Unit Testing Fundamentals 4

    Generalities 4

    Identifying What to Test 6

    The AAA pattern 9

Summary 10

Chapter 2: Clean Code and Clean Architecture for
Easy Unit Testing 11

Clean Code 12

    KISS (Keep It Simple, Stupid) 12

    YAGNI (You Aren't Gonna Need It) 13

    SOLID Principles 14

    Dealing with Private Methods 15

Clean Architecture 16

Summary 26

Chapter 3: Learning the Best Practices with the Best Tools...............27

The Best Tools for the Best Practices..27

    Introducing the Best Tools 27

    Installing the Tools...29

    Taking Advantage of the Best Tools 32

Running Your First Unit Test 68

    Using Visual Studio 69

    Using the CLI 72

Summary..74

Chapter 4: Unit Test .NET Applications 75

Dealing with DataTables 76

Dealing with DateTimes 85

Dealing with Extension Methods..90

    Common Challenges with Extension Methods 90

    The Challenge with ILogger 94

Dealing with Private Methods 99

Dealing with Internal Classes and Methods.......................................103

Dealing with Abstract Classes and Virtual Methods...........................106

Dealing with HttpClients 109

    Testing HttpClient 110

    Testing HttpClient via IHttpClientFactory 113

Dealing with Infrastructure Components 116

Summary..117

Chapter 5: Automating Unit Tests 119

Automate Your Unit Tests in Visual Studio.....................................119

Automate Your Unit Tests in Azure DevOps 125

   What's Azure DevOps?...125

   Getting Started with Azure DevOps 126

   Creating a Continuous Integration Pipeline in Azure DevOps 127

Measure the Code Coverage 141

   Measure the Code Coverage in Visual Studio.............................141

   Measure the Code Coverage in Azure DevOps............................149

   Going Further with the Best Tools...151

Summary...159

Chapter 6: Case Study 161

What Not to Do...161

Refactor Your Application with the Best Practices 165

Unit Test Your Application...177

   Unit Testing the OrderService Class 179

   Unit Testing the OrderValidator Class 187

   Unit Testing the OrderEntityMapper Class 194

Summary...199

Index...201

About the Author

Anthony Giretti is a dedicated developer with two decades of experience and a strong passion for learning new technologies. An eight-time Microsoft MVP and a certified MCSD since 2016, he currently works as an independent senior full-stack developer and architect in Montréal, Canada. Specializing in .NET, his deep expertise in IT and enthusiasm for knowledge sharing empower him to support developers in excelling at their web projects. He thrives on tackling performance constraints, high availability requirements, and optimization challenges.

About the Technical Reviewer

 **Fiodar Sazanavets** is a senior software engineer at Microsoft with over a decade of professional experience. He primarily specializes in .NET and Microsoft stack and is enthusiastic about creating well-crafted software that fully meets business needs. He enjoys teaching aspiring developers and sharing his knowledge with the community, which he has done both as a volunteer and commercially. Fiodar has created several online courses, written a number of technical books, and authored other types of educational content. He also provides live mentoring services, both to groups and individuals. Throughout his career, he has built software of various types and various levels of complexity in multiple industries. This includes a passenger information management system for a railway, distributed smart clusters of IoT devices, ecommerce systems, financial transaction processing systems, and more. He has also successfully led and mentored teams of software developers.

Acknowledgments

This book is not just a culmination of my efforts but a testament to the unwavering support and love of those who stood beside me throughout this journey.

To my incredible wife, Nadege—you were my anchor when the tides of doubt rolled in and my light when the path grew dim. Your faith in me never faltered, and your love gave me the strength to persevere. I love you more than words can ever express.

To my family—you were my foundation and my safe haven. Your encouragement meant the world to me, and I carried your support with me on every page of this book.

And to my dear friend, Fiodar Sazanavets—what a journey it has been! You were not just part of this challenge; you were instrumental in making it possible. Your belief in me and your unwavering camaraderie were essential in reaching this milestone. I cannot thank you enough.

Introduction

You won't believe how many companies I've worked with that struggled with unit testing. Seriously, it's like a universal thing. No matter the size of the company or how complex the project was, they all shared the same issues: messy, unorganized test suites from years of small mistakes piling up, inconsistent testing conventions, outdated tools, and, honestly, some pretty wild misunderstandings of how to design good test cases. It's like testing was an afterthought!

The thing is, I've always loved jumping in and helping teams clean up that mess. It's so satisfying to fix these problems and make testing a breeze! That's why I've decided to write this book. I want to share everything I've learned and help *you* master unit testing. This isn't just a book about theory—I'm diving into practical, hands-on stuff that'll save you from the common headaches developers run into.

By the end of this book, you'll know how to write clean, reliable, and maintainable unit tests that make your applications rock solid. I'm talking about tests that are easy to write and read and don't make you want to pull your hair out. Whether you're just starting or dabbling for a while, you'll come out of this feeling like a pro. Let's level up together!

CHAPTER 1

Introducing Unit Testing Practice

Testing an application reveals errors related to its quality. Whether the test is functional, performance-related, or aimed at verifying the user experience, it's an essential part of software development. The test team (the whole team involved in developing the application, not just the developers) draws up a report on these aspects, enabling the developer to make any necessary corrections. In this chapter you will learn the following:

- Introduction to testing practice
- Unit testing fundamentals

Introduction to Testing Practice

Testing applications early in the development cycle is crucial for identifying and resolving bugs before they have a chance to impact the end user. This proactive approach ensures a smoother, more reliable user experience. In this section, I will provide a brief introduction to the various types of testing you can use to achieve this goal:

- **Unit Testing**: Unit testing focuses on testing individual components or modules of software in isolation. The primary goal is to validate that each unit of functionality behaves as expected, typically using automated tests for faster and repeatable results.

© Anthony Giretti 2025
A. Giretti, *The Unit Testing Practice Cookbook*,
https://doi.org/10.1007/979-8-8688-1454-9_1

- **Integration Testing**: Integration testing verifies that different modules or components of an application work together correctly. For instance, it ensures that the application interacts properly with a database or external APIs, catching issues that might arise when combining independent parts.

- **End-to-End Testing**: End-to-end testing validates the entire workflow of an application, simulating real-world scenarios. It tests the system from start to finish, including interactions with external systems, user interfaces, and back-end services, ensuring that all components work together seamlessly.

- **Functional Testing**: Functional testing examines the application's behavior against defined requirements, focusing on what the software does rather than how it achieves those results. It ensures that specific features or functions produce the correct output based on given inputs.

- **Acceptance Testing**: Acceptance testing evaluates whether the application meets the business requirements and user expectations. The end users or clients often conduct this testing to determine if the product is ready for release and aligns with their needs.

- **Performance Testing**: Performance testing assesses the application's behavior under specific conditions, such as heavy workloads or peak usage times. It focuses on parameters like speed, scalability, and stability, ensuring the system performs optimally under stress.

- **Smoke Testing**: Smoke testing is a preliminary testing phase that checks whether the core functionalities of an application, such as authentication or basic navigation, are working. It acts as a quick health check to determine if the application is stable enough for further testing.

This book is dedicated to unit testing, an essential practice for developers aiming to produce reliable, maintainable code. I won't be addressing integration testing, which is another responsibility for the developer. By concentrating solely on unit testing, this book provides a focused, in-depth exploration of its principles, techniques, and best practices, equipping you with the tools to make it an integral part of your development workflow.

Note   In this book, I am discussing unit testing, which should not be confused with *Test-Driven Development (TDD)*, as they are distinct concepts. Unit testing involves running automated tests on code, typically after the code has been written. In contrast, TDD is an approach where you start by creating unit tests before writing the actual code and then doing this back and forth, coding and continuously running these tests throughout the development process. Test-Driven Development means that you "drive" your development by using a test.

Unit Testing Fundamentals
Generalities

Unit tests enable developers to verify the operation of a unit. A unit of code, known as a *System Under Test (SUT)*, generally a function, contains a particular logic that must be tested without regard to external dependencies. Unit tests are, therefore, performed in **isolation** from the rest of the application, which means, in practice, your test won't connect to any other component or any external data source. This is one of the characteristics of good unit tests, among others:

1. **Repeatable and Deterministic:** The test should produce the same results every time it is run under the same conditions, regardless of the environment or external factors. This ensures reliability and consistency.

2. **Fast**: Unit tests should execute quickly to enable frequent runs during development. Slow tests can hinder productivity and discourage developers from running them regularly.

3. **Readable and Understandable**: A good unit test is easy to read and understand, even for someone unfamiliar with the code. Clear naming conventions, concise test logic, and appropriate comments help achieve this.

4. **Small and Focused**: Each unit test should focus on verifying a specific behavior or functionality, avoiding large, complex test cases. This makes debugging and maintaining the tests easier.

5. **Independent**: Unit tests should not depend on the execution order of other tests or share state with them. Each test should be self-contained and able to run independently.

6. **Verifiable**: The test should clearly define the expected outcome (assertion) and verify that the result matches the expectation. This ensures the purpose of the test is well-defined and measurable.

7. **Maintainable**: A unit test should be easy to update when the code it tests changes. It should avoid hardcoded values or overly specific setups that make maintenance difficult.

8. **Comprehensive Coverage**: Good unit tests cover all critical paths, edge cases, and scenarios relevant to the tested function or component. This reduces the likelihood of undetected bugs.

9. **Fail Clearly**: When a test fails, it should provide clear and actionable feedback, such as which assertion failed and why. This makes debugging faster and more straightforward.

10. **Automatable**: A good unit test should integrate seamlessly into automated test suites, enabling continuous integration and deployment (CI/CD) workflows.

11. **Immediate**: Do your tests right from the start of the project. Otherwise ...you'll never do them! (I say this from experience.)

By adhering to these principles, unit tests can become a powerful tool for ensuring code quality, reducing defects, and improving developer confidence.

Identifying What to Test

Identifyingwhat to test is essential for writing relevant and effective unit tests. It ensures you focus on verifying the most critical aspects of your code, such as expected behaviors, edge cases, and potential failures. By clearly identifying what your SUT is to test and what to test on it, you avoid wasting time on irrelevant tests and instead write targeted ones that catch bugs, validate logic, and maintain code quality. This approach leads to better test coverage, easier debugging, and more confidence in your code's reliability.

Listing 1-1 shows an example of the *Calculator* class, which implements the *Add* method, where two parameters (*a* and *b*, both typed integers) are required for the addition. Your *SUT* is the *Add* method from the *Calculator* class. I'll reuse this class throughout this section.

Listing 1-1. The Calculator class implements the addition of two integers through the Add method

```
public class Calculator
{
    public int Add(int a, int b) => a + b;
}
```

The General Approach to Identifying What to Test on Your SUT

When designing unit tests, consider the following:

- **Parameters**: Understand the range of valid and invalid inputs the method can accept.

- **Output**: Ensure the method produces accurate results and handles edge cases correctly.

- **Dependencies**: Isolate and test interactions with external systems or other methods (through abstractions, or else it's not a unit test), if any.

By following these steps, you ensure your tests are meaningful and address the specific responsibilities of the method, which is about computing an addition between two integers.

Given the *Calculator* class and its *Add* method, let's see what to consider concretely.

Parameters

- **Positive Numbers**: Test the addition of two positive integers to confirm correct behavior.

    Example: Add(3, 5) should return 8.

- **Negative Numbers**: Test the addition of two negative integers to verify the handling of negative values.

    Example: Add(-3, -5) should return -8.

- **Mixed Signs**: Test adding a positive and a negative integer to ensure the result reflects correct subtraction behavior.

    Example: Add(3, -5) should return -2.

- **Boundary Values**: Test extreme cases like Add(int. MaxValue, 1) or Add(int.MinValue, -1) to ensure the method can handle potential overflow scenarios correctly.

The goal here is not just to teach you how to use signed or unsigned numbers but to adapt your tests based on the data type you are working with. For example, if the input were a string, you would test it using string values such as a word, a sentence, or special cases like *null*, "", or *string. Empty*. In C#, a string can have a value, be null, or be empty. Similarly, if the input were a List, you would test it with different scenarios, such as an empty list (new List<T>()), a null list, or a list containing values. A *List<T>* can either be initialized with values, be null, or be empty. Do you understand the reasoning I'm trying to convey? Stay focused—this is fundamental to effective unit testing!

Note   Some functions in your code may not have a return type; for instance, your function could be a *void* or a *Task*. However, this doesn't mean there's nothing to test. You will still need to check the input and the dependencies. I will revisit this topic later in this book.

Output

As mentioned in the "Parameters" subsection, the Add method should always return the sum of the two input integers. Each test verifies that the output matches the expected result for all valid input cases.

Dependencies

This topic does not apply here since the *Calculator* class has no dependencies. I'm trying to start with the unit testing basics in this section. Just keep in mind it's important, and I will develop this aspect later in this book.

The AAA pattern

The *Arrange, Act, Assert (AAA)* pattern is a widely used structure in unit testing that ensures tests are organized, clear, and easy to follow. It consists of three distinct phases.

Arrange, the Preparation Phase

In the *Arrange* phase, all necessary prerequisites for the test are set up. This includes initializing objects, preparing test data, and configuring dependencies (e.g., mocks or stubs; we will discuss that later in this book). The goal is to create the conditions required for the test to execute reliably. Listing 1-2 shows what the *Arrange* phase would look like by instantiating the *Calculator* class and setting up the *Add* function parameters.

Listing 1-2. The Arrange phase is preparing the Calculator class for testing

```
// Arrange: Prepare test objects and data
var calculator = new Calculator(); // Initialize the object to
                                    be tested
int a = 5; // Setting up parameter a
int b = 10; // Setting up parameter b
```

Act, the Execution Phase

The *Act* phase is where the method or function being tested is invoked. This phase is typically concise, focusing solely on calling the code under test with the arranged inputs. Listing 1-3 shows the *Add* function invocation.

Listing 1-3. The Add function during the Act phase

```
// Act: Call the method under test
var result = calculator.Add(a, b);
```

Assert, the Verification Phase

In the *Assert* phase, the outcome of the Act phase is verified against the expected result. Assertions ensure the method behaves as intended, and any deviations are flagged as test failures. Listing 1-4 shows the assertion of the *Add* method outcome.

Listing 1-4. The assertion of the Add method outcome

```
// Assert: Verify the output matches the expected result
Assert.Equal(15, result);
```

As shown, I utilized the *AreEqual* method from the *Assert* static class to compare the expected result with the outcome of the *Add* function. This class is part of the **Microsoft Test SDK**, which I will explain further in this book.

Summary

Congratulations! You are now well-acquainted with the fundamentals of unit testing. These foundational principles are crucial to remember when writing unit tests for your .NET applications. The next chapter will explore how clean coding and architecture principles help write better unit tests!

CHAPTER 2

Clean Code and Clean Architecture for Easy Unit Testing

Clean code and architecture are fundamental for easy unit testing because they help create modular, maintainable, and easy-to-understand software. When code is clean, it is organized so that each component has a clear responsibility, making it easier to isolate and test individual units. This reduces dependencies and makes the testing process more straightforward, as tests can be focused on smaller, well-defined parts of the system. Additionally, a clean architecture ensures that the system is structured to support testing at various levels without making it overly complex or tightly coupled, leading to more efficient and reliable tests. In this chapter, you will learn the following:

- Clean code
- Clean architecture

© Anthony Giretti 2025
A. Giretti, *The Unit Testing Practice Cookbook*,
https://doi.org/10.1007/979-8-8688-1454-9_2

Clean Code

Clean code is a prerequisite for efficient unit testing, and adhering to principles like **KISS** (Keep It Simple, Stupid), **DRY** (Don't Repeat Yourself), **YAGNI** (You Aren't Gonna Need It), and **SOLID** can significantly enhance the testability, maintainability, and clarity of your code. Here's how each of these principles plays a role in making unit testing more efficient.

KISS (Keep It Simple, Stupid)

The *KISS* principle advocates for simplicity in design and implementation. Keeping the code simple is essential for unit testing because of the following reasons:

- **Clear Test Cases**: Simple, straightforward code makes it easier to design meaningful and accurate tests. The less complicated the code, the fewer edge cases and complexities you need to account for in your tests.

- **Reduced Complexity**: When code is simple, the tests also remain simple. Complex, convoluted code requires complicated and harder-to-maintain tests.

Example: Imagine a function handling both user authentication and permission checks. If these responsibilities are mixed, writing unit tests becomes more challenging. By separating the authentication logic, unit tests can be more focused and clear.

DRY (Don't Repeat Yourself)

The *DRY* principle emphasizes eliminating code duplication by abstracting out reusable logic. *DRY* code is beneficial for unit testing for several reasons:

- **Fewer Tests to Maintain**: Redundant code means more places to change if logic changes. By removing duplication, tests are more stable because you won't need to update multiple tests for the same logic.

- **Simpler Test Logic**: Duplicated code often requires the same tests for multiple instances. By following DRY, you reduce the number of places your tests need to cover, making the process more efficient.

Example: If you have validation logic spread across multiple methods, you'd need separate tests for each occurrence. By refactoring to a single method and testing it once, your tests become more streamlined and easier to maintain.

YAGNI (You Aren't Gonna Need It)

The *YAGNI* principle suggests that developers should not add functionality until it is absolutely necessary. This principle helps make unit testing more efficient by

- **Reducing Unnecessary Code**: Unnecessary features or code that you don't need yet just add complexity, making the code harder to test. By following *YAGNI*, you avoid building out unnecessary features that you'll later need to test, leading to cleaner and more focused tests.

- **Focusing on Current Requirements**: Writing code for immediate needs ensures that tests are relevant and only cover the behavior that's actually required right now. This reduces the number of edge cases and complexities that need to be tested.

Example: If you're developing a feature to process orders, you don't need to add complex handling for future features (like a discount system) unless it's part of the current requirement. This allows for simpler unit tests that focus only on the behavior at hand.

SOLID Principles

The *SOLID* principles guide the creation of clean, maintainable, and testable code. Here's how each principle enhances unit testing:

- **S, *Single Responsibility Principle (SRP)***: A class should have only one reason to change, meaning it should focus on one responsibility. This makes testing easier because the behavior is clear and isolated. **Example**: If a class handles both order processing and payment, unit tests become complex as they need to verify both responsibilities. Separating these concerns allows for simpler, focused tests.

- **O, *Open/Closed Principle (OCP)***: Code should be open for extension but closed for modification. This ensures that new features can be added without affecting existing tests or functionality. **Example**: When adding a new feature, following OCP ensures that your tests for existing code remain intact, and only new tests are needed for the new functionality.

- **L, *Liskov Substitution Principle (LSP)***: Derived classes should be able to substitute their base classes without altering correctness. This makes unit testing easier, as you can replace real implementations with mock objects or subclasses during testing.

14

Example: A test that depends on a base class can use a derived class without changing the test behavior, ensuring the test remains predictable and flexible.

- **I, *Interface Segregation Principle (ISP)***: Clients should not be forced to depend on interfaces they don't use. Smaller, more focused interfaces allow tests to mock only the methods that are relevant, making tests more targeted. **Example:** Instead of a large interface with numerous methods, you create smaller, focused interfaces that let you mock only the necessary functionality for each test.

- **D, *Dependency Inversion Principle (DIP)***: High-level modules should not depend on low-level modules but rather on abstractions. This makes the code more modular and testable because dependencies can be substituted with mocks during testing. **Example:** If a service depends on a database, you can replace the real database with a mock repository in your tests, ensuring that tests focus on the service's logic rather than the database.

In particular, *SRP*, *DIP*, and *ISP* promote modular, decoupled code that is easy to test in isolation. In the next subsection, we will go back to them and provide code examples.

Dealing with Private Methods

Private methods can, sometimes, make unit testing difficult because they are not directly accessible outside the class. This forces testers to rely on public methods to trigger private behavior, which may not cover all edge cases or provide fine-grained control. Additionally, testing private methods often requires reflection or altering class design, which can compromise test clarity and maintainability. This reduces the testability of the class and can lead to less effective tests.

Private methods can be replaced with public service injection via dependency injection, as it allows the class to interact with external dependencies in a more testable manner and modularly. This approach makes mock or stub services easier during tests, improving flexibility and isolating behavior for more focused unit tests on the calling method (the method that invokes the private method).

Some developers may disagree with my opinion because private methods are implementation details (of the calling method—I mean the main method that invokes the private method) and should be part of the calling method unit tested. I would say, if you have many private methods or a huge private method that complicates the calling method unit test, create another class that can be unit tested separately and inject in the calling code by dependency injection. If your private(s) don't make your unit test complicated (and do not bother you), unit test your code normally by considering the private code.

In Chapter 6, I will provide concrete case studies and return to private methods there.

Clean Architecture

Unit testing benefits significantly from **clean architecture** because **clean architecture** ensures that the codebase is structured in a way that facilitates isolation, maintainability, and testability. Here's a detailed explanation of why unit testing requires a clean architecture in your applications as a prerequisite:

- **Independence from the User Interface**

  The user interface (e.g., API, desktop application) should operate independently of the core application (business logic, data access, etc.). This book will demonstrate how to use abstraction to decouple your business logic from the user interface.

- **Independence from Third-Party Libraries and Frameworks**

  Avoid tightly coupling your application to specific libraries or frameworks to ensure flexibility and easier technical maintenance. This book will show how to abstract dependencies on third-party tools.

- **Independence from External Data Access**

  Your application should allow easy switching between different types of data sources (e.g., databases, XML files). This book will introduce data access technologies and demonstrate how to achieve flexibility using abstraction.

- **Independent Testability**

  Each layer should be testable in isolation from others. Later in this book, I'll cover unit testing, which also benefits from applying abstraction.

As long as your application meets these requirements, you can choose any shape of **clean architecture** you want that suits your use case. For example, I have witnessed quite a few debates about which architecture to use in a project. Each developer brandished their architecture claiming that their architecture was the best compared with the one proposed by their colleague. These were ultimately sterile debates because everyone was talking about clean architecture but in a different form. We were all ultimately speaking the same language. For example, we were discussing the following architectures:

- Hexagonal architecture

- Onion architecture

- Domain-driven design

These approaches focus on structuring your application's layers (or projects in .NET). I won't go into detail here, as a full explanation would be lengthy and may lead to confusion. Additionally, I aim to avoid reiterating concepts that have already been extensively covered elsewhere. If you want to learn about those architectures, you can find many blog posts about them. Instead, I can propose my own vision of **clean architecture** to you, and I hope it will convince you.

In my approach, an application is divided into at least four layers, as outlined below:

1. **Domain Layer**: This layer contains all domain objects, repository interfaces (for data access), and service interfaces—essentially the application's contracts and abstractions. It is completely independent and does not rely on any other layer.

2. **Presentation Layer**: In this book, the Presentation layer is represented by an ASP.NET Core web layer that exposes APIs over HTTP. While the code in this layer depends only on contracts and abstractions, the application configuration specifies which abstractions are implemented by which concrete classes. This layer depends on all other layers.

3. **Business Logic (or Application) Layer**: This layer implements business rules and orchestrates actions from various components (e.g., data access, logging, caching). It depends solely on the Domain layer, referencing only domain contracts and abstractions. It must not depend on any specific technology or infrastructure. An exception is dependencies on generic helper layers, such as a Tools layer, which can include reusable utilities applicable across multiple scenarios.

4. **Infrastructure Layer(s)**: This layer implements technology-specific details and relies on the Domain layer for abstractions and contracts. It's often useful to have separate Infrastructure layers for each technology (e.g., one for SQL data access and another for HTTP). This modularity ensures flexibility and reusability of individual components.

5. **Optional Tools Layer**: The Tools layer is optional and can include generic, reusable utilities that are independent of application logic or specific technologies. Examples include transforming byte arrays to streams, performing regular expressions, or creating utility classes for common tasks.

To provide a more precise understanding, Figure 2-1 illustrates the interactions between the layers mentioned above, with the *Infrastructure* layers numbered sequentially from 1 to n.

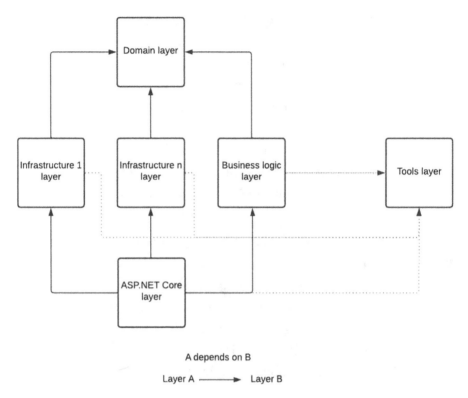

Figure 2-1. *My vision of clean architecture*

As previously mentioned, **clean architecture** ensures that the codebase is designed to facilitate isolation, maintainability, and testability. But how can we achieve this in practice? **Clean architecture** supports unit testing by adhering to the *DIP* discussed earlier. Once again, this principle ensures that high-level modules (e.g., business logic) do not depend on low-level modules (e.g., database or API implementations) but instead rely on abstractions (interfaces). By doing so, you can replace actual implementations with mocks during unit testing, enabling isolation of the code under test.

I have mentioned the term *mock* several times in this chapter, and as promised, it's time to explain what it means:

Mocking is a technique used in unit testing to simulate the behavior of external dependencies, eliminating the need to rely on real implementations. When testing code that depends on external services, databases, or APIs, using the actual dependency in tests is often impractical. Mocking allows you to create a "mock" version of the dependency that can be controlled to return predefined data or behave in specific ways without invoking real external operations.

Mocking behavior involves defining how the mock object should act during the test. For instance, you can configure the mock to return a particular value when a method is called or to throw an exception under specific conditions. This enables you to evaluate how your code handles various scenarios without needing access to the actual dependencies.

Mock data return is a specific mocking aspect where you set up the mock object to return predefined data when a method is called. For example, if your code interacts with a database, you can mock the database call to return specific records or results. This ensures that your tests focus on the logic of your code rather than the actual database interaction, allowing you to test edge cases and failure scenarios in a controlled and predictable environment. It's time to move on to examples. In accordance with the principles of **clean architecture**, we will see together how to architect an order management system in order to make it unit testable.

Listing 2-1 presents the *IOrderRepository* interface (including the *Order* public class), which abstracts the order-saving process and is defined within the **Domain** layer. Following this, Listing 2-2 illustrates the implementation of the *OrderService* class, which takes the *IOrderRepository* interface in the constructor as a dependency. The latter is implemented in the **Business** layer. For simplicity, the abstraction of this class using an *IOrderService* interface in the **Domain** layer is omitted, and the concrete implementation of the *IOrderRepository* interface is also omitted, as the example focuses on abstracting a repository to make

OrderService testable. You might have observed that each interface/class is assigned a single responsibility, in line with the *SRP*. Additionally, the *OrderService* class avoids using unnecessary interfaces, adhering to the *ISP* as well.

Listing 2-1. The IOrderRepository interface and the Order class are defined in the Domain layer

```
// Domain Layer
public interface IOrderRepository
{
    void SaveOrder(Order order);
}

public class Order
{
    public int Id { get; set; }
    public string Product { get; set; }
    public int Quantity { get; set; }
}
```

Listing 2-2. The OrderService class is defined in the Business layer

```
// Business Logic Layer
public class OrderService
{
    private readonly IOrderRepository _orderRepository;

    public OrderService(IOrderRepository orderRepository)
    {
        _orderRepository = orderRepository;
    }

    public void ProcessOrder(Order order)
```

```
{
    if (order.Quantity <= 0)
    {
        throw new Exception("Order quantity must be greater
        than zero.");
    }

    _orderRepository.SaveOrder(order);
}
}
```

I think now you are eager to find out how we are going to unit test the service class, just before I would like to explain three things to you:

In the following example, I'll demonstrate a pattern I often use when writing unit tests: the *When/Should* pattern. This approach focuses on naming test functions in a way that clearly describes both the test conditions (When) and the expected outcome (Should). The naming convention follows this format: *{MethodName}_When{condition}_ Should{expectedBehavior}*. I highly recommend using this pattern as it immediately clarifies the intent of your test, which is essential for creating maintainable and readable unit tests.

Additionally, I'll use the **NSubstitute** mocking library to simulate dependencies, such as the *IOrderRepository* interface, and I'll also use xUnit as the unit test framework. I'll provide a more detailed explanation of this library in the next chapter.

Most importantly, we'll apply the principle discussed earlier in this chapter: clearly identifying what to test. In this case, the *System Under Test (SUT)* is the *ProcessOrder* function in the *OrderService* class. We'll test two key scenarios: (1) when the quantity is less than or equal to 0 and (2) when the quantity is greater than 0. Since 0 is a critical edge case, we'll include an additional test, specifically (3), for this value to ensure no bugs occur when the quantity equals 0. This results in a total of three tests. Listing 2-3 shows this.

Listing 2-3. The `OrderServiceTests` class, which utilizes the NSubstitute library and includes these three tests

```
using NSubstitute; // Mocking library
using Xunit;

namespace Apress.UnitTests;

public class OrderServiceTests
{
    [Fact]
    public void ProcessOrder_WhenQuantityIsGreaterThanZero_
    ShouldInvokeSaveOrder()
    {
        // Arrange
        var mockRepository = Substitute.
        For<IOrderRepository>();
        var orderService = new OrderService(mockRepository);
        var order = new Order { Id = 1, Product = "Book",
        Quantity = 1 };

        // Act
        orderService.ProcessOrder(order);

        // Assert
        mockRepository.Received(1).SaveOrder(order);
// Verifies that SaveOrder was called once with the
specified order
    }

    [Fact]
    public void WhenQuantityEqualsZero_ShouldThrowException()
    {
        // Arrange
```

```csharp
    var mockRepository = Substitute.
    For<IOrderRepository>();
    var orderService = new OrderService(mockRepository);
    var order = new Order { Id = 1, Product = "Book",
    Quantity = 0 };

    // Act & Assert
    Assert.Throws<Exception>(() => orderService.
    ProcessOrder(order));
}

[Fact]
public void WhenQuantityIsLowerThanZero_
ShouldThrowException()
{
    // Arrange
    var mockRepository = Substitute.
    For<IOrderRepository>();
    var orderService = new OrderService(mockRepository);
    var order = new Order { Id = 1, Product = "Book",
    Quantity = -1 };

    // Act & Assert
    Assert.Throws<Exception>(() => orderService.
    ProcessOrder(order));
    }
}
```

As you can see, we have now three tests:

1. For a valid order with a positive quantity

2. For an order with a quantity of 0

3. For an order with a negative quantity

You might have noticed the names of the tests. Don't you think they make the intent of the tests quite clear? 😊

Also, if you take a look at the code, you'll notice that I've used *Substitute.For<T>()* from **NSubstitute** to create a mock of the *IOrderRepository* interface. I then used the *Received(1)* method, also from **NSubstitute**, to check if the *SaveOrder* function was called once. This step is crucial, as we need to ensure that the dependencies are properly invoked to validate the expected behavior. I'll revisit this in the next chapter, where we'll explore the libraries that enhance unit testing. Finally, I also tested whether the *ProcessOrder* method throws an exception when expected, using **NSubstitute**'s *Assert.Throws<T>()* function. I'll go into more detail on this shortly.

After going through this section, don't you think this approach demonstrates how **clean architecture**, *DIP, SRP and ISP* enhance testability while promoting cleaner and more maintainable code? Now, let's move on to the next chapter, where we'll explore some excellent tools that will help you write effective unit tests!

Summary

Clean code and clean architecture are key to efficient unit testing by promoting modular, maintainable, and testable systems. Principles like KISS, DRY, YAGNI, and SOLID encourage simplicity, reduce redundancy, and isolate functionality, making tests easier to write and maintain. Clean architecture structures layers for independence, enabling focused unit testing without external dependencies, while mocking facilitates isolation of the System Under Test. This approach ensures clarity, flexibility, and better test coverage for software components. You are now ready to learn more about the unit test best practices, and we will put them in practice with the best tools in the next chapter!

CHAPTER 3

Learning the Best Practices with the Best Tools

Mastering unit test best practices with the right tools boosts the efficiency and effectiveness of your testing process. Using the appropriate tools helps structure tests, simplify complex scenarios, and ensure consistent results. By applying these practices, you can write clear, maintainable tests that enhance overall code quality. In this chapter, you will learn the following:

- The best tools for the best practices

- Running your first unit test

The Best Tools for the Best Practices

Introducing the Best Tools

To code unit tests efficiently, we'll need several tools and libraries. We'll add the following NuGet packages (on their latest versions):

- **Microsoft.NET.Test.Sdk**: This is a crucial package for running unit tests within a .NET solution. It provides the necessary tools and infrastructure for test

© Anthony Giretti 2025
A. Giretti, *The Unit Testing Practice Cookbook*,
https://doi.org/10.1007/979-8-8688-1454-9_3

execution, making it possible to discover and run tests within the .NET environment.

- **xUnit**: This package allows you to use xUnit as your test framework. It provides a wide range of features, such as running tests in parallel and offering a rich set of assertions and test methods, making it an excellent choice for unit testing in .NET. It's my favorite one among xUnit, NUnit, and MSTest testing frameworks.

- **xunit.runner.visualstudio**: This package integrates xUnit with Visual Studio, enabling the IDE to discover and run your tests seamlessly. Without this package, Visual Studio won't be able to detect or run tests that are written using the xUnit framework, which is critical for smooth test execution and reporting in the Visual Studio environment.

- **NSubstitute**: This is a mocking library for .NET that makes it easier to create substitutes for your dependencies in unit tests. It allows you to isolate the unit of work by mocking interfaces or classes, helping to focus on testing the code's behavior under test rather than the behavior of its dependencies. I always use NSubstitute for its ease of use, but there are also many other libraries like FakeItEasy, Moq, or Rhino Mocks.

- **AutoFixture**: This package simplifies test data generation by automatically creating test objects with randomized or fake data. It helps you populate object properties quickly, saving time and effort to create mock or fake data for your unit tests manually. I can't make any unit test without it!

- **ExpectedObjects**: This package allows you to compare objects based on their values, not just their references. It is beneficial in unit tests when you must compare complex objects and assert that their data matches expected values, making assertions more intuitive and precise—it's a must-have.

- **FluentAssertions**: This one enhances .NET unit testing with a clear, readable syntax using the extension method chaining pattern. It supports deep object and collection comparisons, asynchronous code testing, and exception assertions. The library integrates seamlessly with popular testing frameworks and provides detailed error messages and customization options for maintainable tests. I often qualify it as the cherry on the cake, and I have never regretted using it.

Each package plays a vital role in creating a smooth and efficient unit testing environment, enhancing the testing process with features like mock creation, data generation, and object comparison. To summarize it, they will allow us to write unit tests with the best practices.

Installing the Tools

Microsoft.NET.Test.Sdk

This package is automatically included in any unit test project in Visual Studio. I won't go into detail here. However, you can anyway build your unit test project by creating a simple library and manually adding this package with the following command in the **Package Manager Console**:

```
NuGet\Install-Package Microsoft.NET.Test.Sdk
```

xunit.runner.visualstudio

In Visual Studio, you can create an xUnit test project; the latter will install automatically the **xunit.runner.visualstudio** package as well as the **xunit** package. Figure 3-1 shows the xUnit test project creation in Visual Studio.

Figure 3-1. *xUnit project creation in Visual Studio*

Once the project is created, you will notice in the *csproj* file the packages installed as well as the **Microsoft.NET.Test.Sdk** as shown in Figure 3-2.

```
<ItemGroup>
  <PackageReference Include="coverlet.collector" Version="6.0.0" />
  <PackageReference Include="Microsoft.NET.Test.Sdk" Version="17.8.0" />
  <PackageReference Include="xunit" Version="2.5.3" />
  <PackageReference Include="xunit.runner.visualstudio" Version="2.5.3" />
</ItemGroup>
```

Figure 3-2. *xUnit csproj with the xunit, xunit.runner.visualstudio, and Microsoft.NET.Test.Sdk packages*

You might have noticed the presence of the **coverlet.collector** package as well. Ignore it for now; we will come back to this in Chapter 5. Same as above, you can also create from scratch your test project and install the **xunit.runner.visualstudio** package with the following command:

```
NuGet\Install-Package xunit.runner.visualstudio
```

xUnit

Already installed like the previous package, it can also be installed with the following command:

```
NuGet\Install-Package xunit -Version 2.9.3
```

If you want to read the documentation about it, you can go here and stay updated with the latest releases: `https://xunit.net/`.

NSubstitute

NSubstitute must be installed with the following command since it's not included by default by Visual Studio:

```
NuGet\Install-Package NSubstitute
```

Its documentation can be found at this address: `https://nsubstitute.github.io/help.html`.

AutoFixture

AutoFixture also needs to be installed with the following command since it's not included by default in Visual Studio:

```
NuGet\Install-Package AutoFixture
```

AutoFixture has great documentation that can be found at the following address, in addition to upcoming code samples I'll show you in the next subsection: `https://autofixture.github.io/docs/quick-start/`.

ExpectedObjects

Same again, **ExpectedObjects** is not included by default by Visual Studio and needs to be installed by yourself:

```
NuGet\Install-Package ExpectedObjects
```

ExpectedObjects also has its documentation on GitHub; it could be helpful again along with the code samples I will provide you: https://github.com/derekgreer/expectedObjects/wiki.

FluentAssertions

Same for **FluentAssertions**:

```
NuGet\Install-Package FluentAssertions
```

FluentAssertions also has its documentation, which is very detailed and has many code samples. And it can be found here: https://fluentassertions.com/introduction.

Note   FluentAssertions requires a paid license for versions above 7. If you don't want to pay for a license, you can install the latest free version, which is version 7.1.0.

Taking Advantage of the Best Tools

It is time to introduce you to the main features of the libraries I will be using throughout this book. Of course, I won't cover all the features of each library; I don't want you to feel overwhelmed. I will show you everything that I consider essential. After showing you basic examples of each library, in the next section, we will go into Visual Studio to run these examples to show you how it works (with Visual Studio and with the Command Line Interface (CLI)). Let's start now with xUnit.

xUnit

xUnit relies on some attributes to discover and run the tests. This is where the *Fact* and *Theory* attributes come in. Let me give more explanations.

The Fact Attribute

The *Fact* attribute marks methods that are **simple tests** with **no input parameters**. Without the *Fact* attribute, xUnit won't know that the method is a test to execute. In addition, a *Fact* method tests a fixed condition or behavior. It implies that the test doesn't require parameters and will run in isolation, making it straightforward and self-contained. xUnit will treat this method as a "single test" executed independently when you run your tests. Listing 3-1 shows the *StringTests* class that implements the *WhenInputIsNull_ShouldReturnTrue* test method where a string is tested and returns **true** if its data is null. The tested method (the *SUT*) is the *string.IsNullOrEmpty* static method. Once again, ignore the *Assert.True* method, for now; I'll go back to this very soon.

Listing 3-1. The string.IsNullOrEmpty method tested against a null value within the WhenInputIsNull_ShouldReturnTrue test method

```
using System;
using Xunit;

namespace Apress.UnitTests;

public class StringTests
{
    [Fact]
    public void IsNullOrEmpty_WhenInputIsNull_
    ShouldReturnTrue()
    {
        // Arrange
```

```
        string input = string.Empty;

        // Act
        bool result = string.IsNullOrEmpty(input);

        // Assert
        Assert.True(result);
    }
}
```

In this example, the *IsNullOrEmpty_WhenInputIsNull_ ShouldReturnTrue* method is self-contained and doesn't take any parameters, so it uses the *Fact* attribute.

If you want to skip the execution of a test (don't want to run it, and leave it as ignored), you can use the property *Skip* on the *Fact* attribute as follows:

```
[Fact (Skip = "specific reason")]
```

This is particularly useful when your test doesn't work and you want to put it on the side and take care of all other tests. It often happens to me; don't hesitate to use it if you don't want to keep pulling your hair ☺.

You may want to test every possible scenario, and you are right because the *SUT (string.IsNullOrEmpty)* can return **true** when the string input is null or empty. How do you test that with a single test? This is how the *Theory* attribute comes in.

The Theory Attribute

The *Theory* attribute works with another attribute named *InlineData*. Listing 3-2 shows the *IsNullOrEmpty_WhenInputIsNullOrEmpty_ ShouldReturnTrue* test method within the *StringTests* class testing whether *null* or "" makes the test succeed by using the *Theory* and *InlineData* attributes.

Listing 3-2. The string.IsNullOrEmpty method tested against a null and an empty value within the IsNullOrEmpty_ WhenInputIsNullOrEmpty_ShouldReturnTrue test method

```
using System;
using Xunit;

namespace Apress.UnitTests;

public class StringTests
{
    [Theory]
    [InlineData(null)]
    [InlineData("")]
    public void IsNullOrEmpty_WhenInputIsNullOrEmpty_
    ShouldReturnTrue(string input)
    {
        // Act
        bool result = string.IsNullOrEmpty(input);

        // Assert
        Assert.True(result);
    }
}
```

In this case, the *Fact* attribute is replaced by the *Theory* attribute, which allows xUnit to discover the test. You can also see that *WhenInputIsNullOrEmpty_ShouldReturnTrue* is parameterized. This enables xUnit to run the test multiple times—specifically, twice— because the *InlineData* attribute is used to provide different parameters. Each parameter will trigger a separate test execution using the corresponding value.

From this example, I would like to show you something I'm not a fan of practicing in unit testing. If you remember, earlier in this book,

35

I mentioned that unit tests should be deterministic and specific. The following example shows a test that does not follow these best practices (it's my opinion, and it's not the absolute truth; other developers could disagree). With xUnit and its *Theory* and *InlineData* attributes, it would be tempting to create a single test to check all possible cases: a null string, an empty string, or a string with a value. Listing 3-3 shows the test **IsNullOrEmpty_WhenInputIsProvided_ShouldReturnTheRightResult** using all possible cases for the function *string.IsNullOrEmpty*, which returns true for inputs that are null or empty and **false** if a non-null, non-empty value is provided. The parameter used for this is the *expectedResult* parameter.

Listing 3-3. The string.IsNullOrEmpty method tested against a null, an empty, and a non-empty value within the IsNullOrEmpty_ WhenInputIsProvided_ShouldReturnTheRightResult test method

```
using System;
using Xunit;

namespace Apress.UnitTests;

public class StringTests
{
    [Theory]
    [InlineData(null, true)]
    [InlineData("", true)]
    [InlineData("hello", false)]
    public void IsNullOrEmpty_WhenInputIsProvided_ShouldReturnT
    heRightResult(string input, bool expectedResult)
    {
        // Act
        bool result = string.IsNullOrEmpty(input);
```

```
    // Assert
    Assert.Equals(expectedResult, result);
  }
}
```

The test will pass, but you'll realize that it is not meaningful because the name of the test method is not very descriptive and the test's intent is unclear. Secondly, the test evaluates two behaviors: a true result and a false result. To address this, the best practice would be to create two tests: one that tests a true result with null and empty values and another test that tests a false result by passing a non-empty parameter. Listing 3-4 shows the final implementation of the test class *StringTests* with two test functions, *WhenInputIsNullOrEmpty_ShouldReturnTrue* and *WhenInputIsNotEmpty_ ShouldReturnFalse.*

Listing 3-4. The string.IsNullOrEmpty method tested against a null and an empty value within the IsNullOrEmpty_ WhenInputIsNullOrEmpty_ShouldReturnTrue test method and a non-empty value within the IsNullOrEmpty_ WhenInputIsNotEmpty_ShouldReturnFalse test method

```
using System;
using Xunit;

namespace Apress.UnitTests;

public class StringTests
{
    [Theory]
    [InlineData(null)]
    [InlineData("")]
    public void IsNullOrEmpty_WhenInputIsNullOrEmpty_
    ShouldReturnTrue(string input)
```

```
    {
        // Act
        bool result = string.IsNullOrEmpty(input);

        // Assert
        Assert.True(result);
    }

    [Fact]
    public void WhenInputIsNotEmpty_ShouldReturnFalse()
    {
        // Arrange
        string input = "hello";

        // Act
        bool result = string.IsNullOrEmpty(input);

        // Assert
        Assert.False(result);
    }
}
```

This basic example shows you concretely what a deterministic test focused on a single behavior is. I will reuse this principle throughout this book; it is a key point in unit testing.

Another interesting aspect of xUnit is the use of constructors. xUnit can execute tests independent of each other, even if it has a constructor. In complex unit testing scenarios, we use shared elements like mocks or variables to avoid rewriting them in each test method, for readability purposes. The constructor will be invoked with each test execution. Listing 3-5 shows a class member named myNumber, which is shared between two test methods (*WhenOneIsAddedToOne_ShouldReturnTwo* and *WhenOneIsSubtractedFromOne_ShouldReturnZero*), where one performs addition and the other subtraction, without any collision between the test methods. The addition and subtraction will thus give the expected result.

Listing 3-5. The WhenOneIsAddedToOne_ShouldReturnTwo and the WhenOneIsSubtractedFromOne_ShouldReturnZero modifying both the myNumber class member

```
using Xunit;

namespace Apress.UnitTests;

public class ComputeTests
{
    private int myNumber;

    public ComputeTests()
    {
        myNumber = 1;
    }

    [Fact]
    public void WhenOneIsAddedToOne_ShouldReturnTwo()
    {
        // Arrange
        int valueToAdd = 1;
        // Act
        myNumber += valueToAdd;

        // Assert
        Assert.Equal(2, myNumber);
    }

    [Fact]
    public void WhenOneIsSubstractedFromOne_ShouldReturnZero()
```

```
    {
        // Arrange
        int valueToSubstract = 1;

        // Act
        myNumber -= valueToSubstract;

        // Assert
        Assert.Equal(0, myNumber);
    }
}
```

The result of these two tests will be as expected. The addition will give the result of two, while the subtraction will give zero. If there had been any collision, these tests would not have worked. I will come back to this later in this book when I show you concrete examples.

The last important aspect in xUnit is assertions. I teased them a bit earlier in this book, and now I will present them to you in Table 3-1.

Table 3-1. *The main methods of the* Assert *class in xUnit, along with a brief description of their purpose*

Method	Description
Assert.Equal(expected, actual)	Verifies that the two values are equal
Assert.NotEqual(expected, actual)	Verifies that the two values are not equal
Assert.True(condition)	Verifies that the condition is true
Assert.False(condition)	Verifies that the condition is false
Assert.Null(object)	Verifies that the object is null
Assert.NotNull(object)	Verifies that the object is not null

(continued)

Table 3-1. (*continued*)

Method	Description
Assert.Empty(collection)	Verifies that the collection is empty
Assert.NotEmpty(collection)	Verifies that the collection is not empty
Assert.Contains(collection, element)	Verifies that an element exists in the collection
Assert.DoesNotContain (collection, element)	Verifies that an element does not exist in the collection
Assert.Throws<TException> (action)	Verifies that an exception of type TException is thrown during the execution of the action
Assert.ThrowsAny<TException> (action)	Verifies that an exception of any type TException is thrown during the execution of the action
Assert.Raises<TException> (action)	Verifies that a specific exception is raised during the execution of an action
Assert.Single(collection)	Verifies that the collection contains exactly one element
Assert.InRange(value, low, high)	Verifies that the value is within the specified range (between low and high)
Assert.NotInRange(value, low, high)	Verifies that the value is not within the specified range (between low and high)
Assert.Same(expected, actual)	Verifies that the two objects refer to the same object in memory (reference comparison)
Assert.NotSame(expected, actual)	Verifies that the two objects do not refer to the same object in memory

These methods are core tools for making assertions in unit tests with xUnit. They allow you to verify different conditions and ensure the code behaves as expected. In this book, I will replace them with the FluentAssertions library, but it does not mean you have to do the same; FluentAssertions is my favorite tool for assertions. However, the xUnit assertion methods are perfectly fine. It's up to you!

FluentAssertions

FluentAssertions is a great alternative to xUnit (and MSTest) assertion methods because it provides a more expressive, readable, and flexible syntax. While xUnit assertions are straightforward, FluentAssertions offers several advantages:

1. **Fluent API**: FluentAssertions uses a fluent API, allowing you to chain assertions together in a more readable and natural way. This often leads to more descriptive and clear tests.

2. **Better Error Messages**: FluentAssertions provides detailed and clear error messages, which make it easier to understand why a test failed. This can save time and make debugging more efficient.

3. **Additional Assertions**: FluentAssertions includes more specialized assertions than xUnit by default. It provides support for a wide range of object comparisons, collection assertions, exception handling, and more.

4. **Readability**: The syntax often reads more like natural language, improving the clarity of tests. This can be especially helpful when working in teams, as it reduces the need to explain assertions.

Listing 3-6 shows the *Person* class that will be unit tested.

Listing 3-6. The Person class

```
namespace Apress.UnitTests.Models;

public class Person
{
    public string FirstName { get; private set; }
    public string LastName { get; private set; }
    public string FullName { get; private set; }

    public Person(string firstname, string lastname)
    {
        FirstName = firstname;
        LastName = lastname;
        FullName = string.Concat(firstname, " ",lastname);
    }
}
```

Note   I voluntarily chose to use classes over Struct or Record for the Person class. The reason is I want to teach you further how to deal with classes passed as parameters of methods. Classes are reference types, while Structs are value types. Records are reference types, but comparing them with other records is made by value.

As you may have guessed, we will unit test the correct instantiation of the *Person* class by verifying the *FirstName, LastName,* and *FullName* properties.

Listing 3-7 shows the *PersonTests* test class with its *Person_ WhenPersonIsCorrectlyInstantiated_ShouldReturnFirstNameAndLastName AndFullNameCorrectlyFilled* test method.

43

> **Note**   The test method name might seem a bit long, but it's not considered bad practice, as it still adheres to the deterministic criteria for the unit test practice. Additionally, when I'm not testing a method, I put the class name at the beginning of the test name; here I have used the *Person* class name.

Listing 3-7. The PersonTests test class

```
using Apress.UnitTests.Models;
using FluentAssertions;
using Xunit;

namespace Apress.UnitTests;

public class PersonTests
{
    [Fact]
    public void Person_WhenPersonIsCorrectlyInstantiated_
    ShouldReturnFirstNameAndLastNameAndFullNameCorrectlyFilled()
    {
        // Arrange
        var person = new Person("Anthony", "Giretti");

        // Assert
        person.FirstName.Should().Be("Anthony");
        person.LastName.Should().Be("Giretti");
        person.FullName.Should().Be("Anthony Giretti");

        // Comparing with xUnit assertions
        Assert.Equal("Anthony", person.FirstName);
        Assert.Equal("Giretti", person.LastName);
```

```
    Assert.Equal("Anthony Giretti", person.FullName);
  }
}
```

As you can see, I provided the assertions using both FluentAssertions and xUnit. As I've mentioned, I prefer FluentAssertions, but what do you prefer to use? In any case, there's no wrong choice. The last thing essential to mention here is that I made three assertions. Writing several assertions in the same test does not mean testing several behaviors. Here, I tested the **same behavior**: the correct instantiation of the *Person* class!

To go a little bit more forward with FluentAssertions, I want to show you, in Table 3-2, the main methods provided by FluentAssertions.

Table 3-2. *The main methods provided by FluentAssertions, along with a brief description of their purpose*

Method	Description
Should().Be(value)	Verifies that the object is equal to the expected value
Should().NotBe(value)	Verifies that the object is not equal to the expected value
Should().BeNull()	Verifies that the object is null
Should().NotBeNull()	Verifies that the object is not null
Should().BeGreaterThan(value)	Verifies that the object is greater than the given value
Should().BeLessThan(value)	Verifies that the object is less than the given value
Should().Contain(substring)	Verifies that a string contains the specified substring
Should().NotContain(substring)	Verifies that a string does not contain the specified substring

(continued)

Table 3-2. (*continued*)

Method	Description
Should().HaveCount(count)	Verifies that a collection has the expected number of elements
Should().BeEmpty()	Verifies that a collection or string is empty
Should().HaveLength(length)	Verifies that a string or collection has the specified length
Should().Throw<TException>()	Verifies that the specified exception type is thrown when an action is executed
Should().NotThrow()	Verifies that no exception is thrown when an action is executed
Should().Match(regex)	Verifies that the string matches the specified regular expression
Should().ContainEquivalent Of(value)	Verifies that the collection contains an element equivalent to the specified value
Should().BeOfType<T>()	Verifies that the object is of the expected type T
Should().NotBeOfType<T>()	Verifies that the object is not of the expected type T
Should().BeApproximately (value)	Verifies that a floating-point value is approximately equal to the expected value within a tolerance
Should().BeInRange(min, max)	Verifies that the value is within the specified range
Should().NotBeInRange(min, max)	Verifies that the value is not within the specified range

As you can see, FluentAssertions provides a comprehensive API that can enhance the readability of your unit tests. I won't cover all of its features in this book; this list is simply to familiarize you with FluentAssertions' capabilities. It should also help you decide between using it or xUnit assertions. :)

FluentAssertions also supports chained assertions by using the And keyword as follows:

```
person.FullName.Should().Contain("Anthony").And.Contain
("Giretti");
```

Isn't that practical? ☺

AutoFixture

AutoFixture can automatically generate test data for your unit tests. This is especially useful when the objects you're testing have many properties, particularly when those properties don't significantly impact the test. I use AutoFixture whenever possible to save time and improve the readability of my unit tests—less code often means clearer tests. AutoFixture generates data automatically based on property types and allows developers to customize property values or even ignore them (set them to null), making it highly flexible. I'll use a class named *Address*, which contains many properties, and a method named *Display*, which takes the *Person* class as a parameter. Then, I will unit test the *Display* method, my *SUT* here. Listing 3-8 shows the *Address* class.

Listing 3-8. The Address class

```
namespace Apress.UnitTests.Models;

public class Address
{
    public string Street { get; set; }
    public int StreetNumber { get; set; }
    public string City { get; set; }
    public string State { get; set; }
    public string ZipCode { get; set; }
    public string Country { get; set; }
```

```
public string ApartmentNumber { get; set; }

public string Display(Person person)
{
    var aptNumber = !string.IsNullOrWhiteSpace(Apartment
    Number) ? $" {ApartmentNumber}" : string.Empty;
    // Format the address as a readable string
    return $"{person.FullName} lives at {StreetNumber}
{Street}{aptNumber}, {City}, {State}, {ZipCode}, {Country}";
}
}
```

Let's assume the *ApartmentNumber* property could be null (it could also be empty or have whitespaces, but let's focus on the null value), which would affect the behavior of the *Display* method. The method has two possible behaviors: displaying the address with the *ApartmentNumber* and displaying it without the *ApartmentNumber* when it is null. Now, let's see how AutoFixture can simplify unit tests on the *AddressTests* class that implements two test methods: *Display_WhenAddressIsSetWithApartmentNumber_ ShouldDisplayAddressWithApartmentNumberCorrectly* and the *Display_When AddressIsNotSetWithApartmentNumber_ShouldDisplayAddressWithout ApartmentNumberCorrectly* methods, as demonstrated in Listing 3-9:

Listing 3-9. The AddressTests class

```
using Apress.UnitTests.Models;
using AutoFixture;
using FluentAssertions;
using System.Diagnostics.Metrics;
using Xunit;

namespace Apress.UnitTests;

public class AddressTests
```

```
{
    private readonly Fixture _fixture;

    public AddressTests()
    {
        _fixture = new Fixture();
    }

    [Fact]
    public void Display_WhenAddressIsSetWithApartmentNumber_
    ShouldDisplayAddressWithApartmentNumberCorrectly()
    {
        // Arrange
        var address = _fixture.Build<Address>()
                            .With(x => x.Country, "Canada")
                            .Create();
        var person = _fixture.Create<Person>();

        // Act
        var displayedAddress = address.Display(person);

        // Assert
        displayedAddress.Should().Be($"{person.FullName} lives
        at {address.StreetNumber} {address.Street} {address.
        ApartmentNumber}, {address.City}, {address.State},
        {address.ZipCode}, {address.Country}");
    }

    [Fact]
    public void Display_WhenAddressIsNotSetWithApartment
    Number_ShouldDisplayAddressWithoutApartmentNumberCorrectly()
```

```
{
    var address = _fixture.Build<Address>()
                    .Without(x => x.ApartmentNumber)
                    .Create();
    var person = _fixture.Create<Person>();

    // Act
    var displayedAddress = address.Display(person);
    // Assert
    displayedAddress.Should().Be($"{person.FullName} lives
    at {address.StreetNumber} {address.Street}, {address
    .City}, {address.State}, {address.ZipCode}, {address
    .Country}");
}
}
```

As you can see, I've instantiated an object of type *Fixture*, which is the core class of AutoFixture. Since it's used in both test methods, I'll initialize it in the constructor of the *AddressTests* class. Both test methods use AutoFixture to generate an *Address* object and a *Person* object. The *Display_WhenAddressIsSetWithApartmentNumber_ ShouldDisplayAddressWithApartmentNumberCorrectly* test method uses the *Build* function to create an *Address* object, customizing it with the *With* method to set "Canada" as the value for the *Country* property. The *Build* method is necessary when you want to customize your object either by utilizing the *With* or *Without* method before calling the *Create* method. With the exception of the *Country* property, the other properties of the *Address* object are generated randomly. The main advantage of using AutoFixture is that it enables you to easily generate data without worrying about specific values, which is exactly what we need here. Our goal is to simply verify that the displayed address correctly reflects the properties of the *Address* object. I used a specific value for the *Country* property just for demonstration purposes.

In the *Display_WhenAddressIsNotSetWithApartmentNumber_ ShouldDisplayAddressWithoutApartmentNumberCorrectly* test method, I used the *Without* method to customize the *ApartmentNumber* property. The *Without* method sets specified properties to null, while the other properties are generated randomly. In this case, we want to test if the address is correctly displayed when the *ApartmentNumber* is missing (i.e., set to null).

From this example, you can see that AutoFixture allows you to focus on testing the logic of the *Display* method rather than spending time on data setup, which is kept to a minimum. This library is essential in my opinion, and I hope I've convinced you to incorporate it into your unit tests.

Lastly, AutoFixture provides other possibilities, for example:

- **Collection and List Creation**:

  - **Purpose**: Generates multiple instances of a specified type

  - **Method**: fixture.CreateMany<T>()

  - **Example**: `var people = fixture.CreateMany <Person>(5);`

- **Freezing Values**:

  - **Purpose**: Allows you to "freeze" a specific value for a given type, so the same value is used across multiple object creations in the same test

  - **Method**: fixture.Freeze<T>()

  - **Example**: `var frozenPerson = fixture. Freeze<Person>();`

Another great reason to use AutoFixture, particularly with collections, is that it can save you significant time!

NSubstitute

Mocking is crucial when using interfaces in a class because it allows you to isolate and test specific behaviors without depending on the actual implementation of the interface. This is especially important for unit tests, where you want to focus on testing the logic of your class in isolation.

By mocking an interface, you can simulate different scenarios (such as specific method calls, exceptions, or return values) and verify how your class interacts with the interface. This ensures your tests are more reliable and faster and don't require actual dependencies or side effects (like database calls, file access, or network requests). Mocking helps to test the class behavior under controlled conditions and ensures that it behaves correctly regardless of external factors.

NSubstitute is a popular .NET mocking library used to create mock objects for unit testing. It allows for easy stubbing of methods, properties, and events with minimal boilerplate code. Key methods include the *Substitute.For<T>* method to create mocks, *Returns* to specify method return values, *DidNotReceive* to verify that a method was not called, *Received* to verify how many times a method was called, and *Arg.Is<T>* to test specific parameters passed to methods. If the parameter value is not important to get tested, I'll show you in what condition it makes sense; you can replace the *Arg.Is<T>* by the *Arg.Any<T>* method.

We will put into practice the use of these methods with Listings 3-10, 3-11, and 3-12. Listing 3-10 shows the *User class*, which contains the properties *Id, FirstName, LastName, Email*, and *IsActive*. Listing 3-11 represents the *IUserRepository* interface, which contains a single asynchronous method: *GetByIdAsync*, which returns a *User* object. Listing 3-12 represents the *UserService* class, where the *IUserRepository* interface is injected. It then implements a method that we will unit test: *GetById*, which takes a user *id* as a parameter and returns a *User* object.

Listing 3-10. The User class

```
namespace Apress.UnitTests.Models;

public class User
{
    public int Id { get; set; }
    public string FirstName { get; set; }
    public string LastName { get; set; }
    public string Email { get; set; }
    public bool IsActive { get; set; }
}
```

Listing 3-11. The IUserRepository interface

```
using Apress.UnitTests.Models;

namespace Apress.UnitTests.Interfaces;

public interface IUserRepository
{
    Task<User> GetByIdAsync(int id);
}
```

Listing 3-12. The UserService class

```
using Apress.UnitTests.Interfaces;
using Apress.UnitTests.Models;

namespace Apress.UnitTests.Services;

public class UserService
{
    private readonly IUserRepository _userRepository;

    public UserService(IUserRepository userRepository)
```

```
    {
        _userRepository = userRepository;
    }

    public async Task<User> GetById(int id)
    {
        if (id > 0)
            return await _userRepository.GetByIdAsync(id);
        return await Task.FromResult<User>(null);
    }
}
```

As you can see, the *GetById* method has two possible scenarios:

1. If the *id* parameter is greater than 0 (a valid, positive integer), it calls the *GetByIdAsync* method of the *IUserRepository* interface to fetch the corresponding *User* object asynchronously.

2. If the *id* parameter is 0 or less (which is considered invalid), the method returns null by using *Task. FromResult<User>(null)*. This returns a completed task with a null result, which is necessary because the method is asynchronous, but no actual data is returned in this case.

You may have guessed it—we will have four unit tests to write, two for each method. Well, not exactly. For the *GetById* method, one test might seem unnecessary to perform. It's testing what happens when the *IUserRepository* returns null. We want to ensure that the repository was indeed called with the right parameters, even if the *GetByIdAsync* method in the *UserService* class returns null. You didn't see that one coming, did you? Well, we will actually have five tests in total.

> **Tip** Unit tests for mock calls verify that your code interacts correctly with dependencies by ensuring the right methods are invoked with the expected parameters. They help isolate the unit under test, catching errors early (like hardcoded parameters or parameter changes) and preventing regressions.This approach enhances overall code reliability.

The same reasoning applies to the *GetUserByStatusAsync* method (except the fact it could return null or an empty collection), and you can do it yourself if you've understood the logic I'm trying to instill: handle the edge cases! Listing 3-13 shows the *UserServiceTests* class that embeds the *GetById* method unit test.

Listing 3-13. The UserServiceTests class

```
using Apress.UnitTests.Interfaces;
using Apress.UnitTests.Models;
using Apress.UnitTests.Services;
using AutoFixture;
using FluentAssertions;
using NSubstitute;
using Xunit;

namespace Apress.UnitTests;

public class UserServiceTests
{
    private readonly Fixture _fixture;
    private readonly IUserRepository _userRepositoryMock;
    private readonly UserService _sut;

    public UserServiceTests()
```

```
    {
        _fixture = new Fixture();
        _userRepositoryMock = Substitute.For<IUserRepository>();
        _sut = new UserService(_userRepositoryMock);
        _fixture.Customizations.Add(new RandomNumericSequence
        Generator(1, int.MaxValue));
    }

    [Fact]
    public async Task GetByIdAsync_WhenIdIsLowerOrEquals
    Zero_ShouldReturnNullAndRepositoryShouldNotBeInvoked()
    {
        // Arrange
        _fixture.Customizations.Clear();
        _fixture.Customizations.Add(new RandomNumericSequence
        Generator(int.MinValue, 0));
        var id = _fixture.Create<int>();

        // Act
        var user = await _sut.GetByIdAsync(id);

        // Assert
        user.Should().BeNull();
        await _userRepositoryMock.DidNotReceive().GetByIdAsync
        (Arg.Any<int>());
    }

    [Fact]
    public async Task GetByIdAsync_WhenIdIsGreaterThan
    Zero_ShouldReturnUserObjectAndRepositoryShouldBeInvoked
    WithTheRightParameters()
```

```csharp
{
    // Arrange
    var id = _fixture.Create<int>();
    var user = _fixture.Create<User>();
    _userRepositoryMock.GetByIdAsync(Arg.Any<int>())
    .Returns(user);

    // Act
    var result = await _sut.GetByIdAsync(id);

    // Assert
    user.Should().Be(user);
    await _userRepositoryMock.Received(1).GetByIdAsync
    (Arg.Is(id));
}

[Fact]
public async Task GetByIdAsync_WhenIdIsGreaterThan
ZeroAndUserRepositoryReturnsNull_ShouldReturnNull()
{
    // Arrange
    var id = _fixture.Create<int>();
    _userRepositoryMock.GetByIdAsync(Arg.Any<int>())
    .Returns((User)null);

    // Act
    var user = await _sut.GetByIdAsync(id);

    // Assert
    user.Should().BeNull();
    await _userRepositoryMock.Received(1).GetByIdAsync
    (Arg.Is(id));
}
}
```

Let's go in some explanations:

Regarding the constructor and the private variables, the _userRepositoryMock_ variable is a mocked version of the _IUserRepository_ interface using NSubstitute. The constructor initializes the fixture, repository mock, and the _UserService_ instance. A custom sequence generator (_RandomNumericSequenceGenerator_) is added to AutoFixture for generating a sequence of random integers within a specified range to help with generating random values for integer-type properties.

Regarding the _GetByIdAsync_WhenIdIsLowerOrEqualsZero_ ShouldReturnNullAndRepositoryShouldNotBeInvoked_ test method, the _id_ is randomly generated within a range that includes zero and negative numbers (using _RandomNumericSequenceGenerator_). I'm not using the one defined in the constructor since the latter is used for the two other tests that need to use positive numbers. Then, the _GetByIdAsync_ method is called with this id.

Assertion 1: The returned user should be null because the _GetByIdAsync_ method should return null for invalid ids.

Assertion 2: The repository method (_GetByIdAsync_) should not be invoked at all, as the method should return null without interacting with the repository when the id is invalid; for this I'm using the _DidNotReceive_ method from NSubstitute. I'm using the _Arg.Any<int>_ parameter, since we don't need to test a specific value as parameter (since the repository is not called).

Expected Behavior: For invalid ids, the repository should not be called, and the method should return null.

Regarding the _GetByIdAsync_WhenIdIsGreaterThanZero_Should ReturnUserObjectAndRepositoryShouldBeInvokedWithTheRight Parameters_ test method, a random positive id is generated using AutoFixture. A mock _User_ object is created using AutoFixture to simulate a valid user, and the _GetByIdAsync_ method of the repository is mocked to return (with the _Returns_ method) the created user when called with any int value. Then, the _GetByIdAsync_ method is called with the valid id.

Assertion 1: The returned user should match the mocked user object.

Assertion 2: The *GetByIdAsync* method of the repository should be invoked once, and it should be invoked with the correct id (using *Arg. Is(id)*).

Expected Behavior: The repository method should be invoked with the correct id, and the method should return the mocked *User* object.

Regarding the *GetByIdAsync_WhenIdIsGreaterThanZeroAndUser RepositoryReturnsNull_ShouldReturnNull* test method, the reasoning is the same as the previous test method, except the fact we check the behavior when the repository returns null.

These examples highlight an important principle I mentioned before: testing one behavior at a time, with each behavior being covered by a separate unit test. The more you progress through this book, the more you'll realize how much sense it makes.

To finish with NSubstitute, you've probably noticed that NSubstitute can handle all possible situations. I haven't shown you everything because this library is huge, and I recommend reading their documentation—it's really well done. However, I'll show you another use case that occurs more often than you might think. For example, let's consider that we want to mock the behavior of an interface, but this interface (and its method) gets invoked multiple times. How do we handle that? With NSubstitute, it's easy to do. Listing 3-14 shows the *DeleteByIdsAsync* service method, which calls the *IUserRepository*'s *DeleteByIdAsync* method multiple times in a loop and returns an integer. The *DeleteByIdsAsync* method returns true when all users have been deleted and false if not. Note that the *DeleteByIdAsync* repository method returns 1 when the user is deleted and 0 when it's not.

Listing 3-14. The DeleteByIdsAsync service method

```
public async Task<bool> DeleteByIdsAsync(IEnumerable<int> ids)
{
    foreach(int id in ids)
        if (await _userRepository.DeleteByIdAsync(id) == 0)
            return false;
    return true;
}
```

Let's assume we have a list of two ids where one is deleted and the other is not (generated with the *CreateMany<T>* method from AutoFixture). Naturally, we need to test the output, which should return false. We'll mock the two calls (*DeleteByIdAsync* repository method), making one return 1 and the other return 0. Listing 3-15 shows the test method *DeleteByIdAsync_WhenAListOfUserIdIsProvidedAndSomeAre NotDeleted_ShouldReturnFalseAndInvokeDeleteByIdAsyncForEachUserId*, which performs this test.

Listing 3-15. The DeleteByIdAsync_WhenAListOfUserIdIsProvided AndSomeAreNotDeleted_ShouldReturnFalseAndInvokeDelete ByIdAsyncForEachUserId test method

```
[Fact]
public async Task DeleteByIdAsync_
WhenAListOfUserIdIsProvidedAndSomeAreNotDeleted_
ShouldReturnFalseAndInvokeDeleteByIdAsyncForEachUserId()
{
    // Arrange
    var ids = _fixture.CreateMany<int>(2);
    var firstId = ids.First();
    var lastId = ids.Last();
    _userRepositoryMock.DeleteByIdAsync(Arg.Is(firstId)).
```

```
Returns(1); _userRepositoryMock.DeleteByIdAsync(Arg.
Is(lastId)).Returns(0);

    // Act
    var result = await _sut.DeleteByIdsAsync(ids);

    // Assert
    result.Should().BeFalse();
    await _userRepositoryMock.Received(1).DeleteByIdAsync(Arg.
    Is(firstId));
    await _userRepositoryMock.Received(1).DeleteByIdAsync(Arg.
    Is(lastId));
}
```

As you can see, I apply the same principle as before, using NSubstitute's *Returns* function to define the behavior of the repository method *DeleteByIdAsync*. To differentiate between the two calls and their behaviors, I must identify them using the parameters passed as arguments with *Arg.Is*, rather than *Arg.Any*, because the parameter values cannot be omitted. The first call returns 1, and the second returns 0. Then, we execute the test and use the *Received(1)* method with the *Arg.Is* argument to verify that each call was made once with the correct argument.

I will stop here with the NSubstitute examples; I'll revisit it in the upcoming chapters, but also in the next section, as it can work in synergy with ExpectedObjects.

ExpectedObjects

ExpectedObjects and NSubstitute together provide a powerful combination for unit testing. Here's why:

1. **Simplifies Object Comparisons**

   ExpectedObjects allows for more concise and
   readable object comparisons. Instead of manually
   comparing the properties of an object in each test,
   you can rely on the *ToExpectedObject* method to
   easily define and compare an expected version of an
   object. This is particularly useful when dealing with
   complex objects that contain multiple properties
   or nested objects. Instead of manually checking
   each field or property in your assertions, you can let
   ExpectedObjects handle the comparison.

2. **Seamless Integration with NSubstitute**

   NSubstitute is great for mocking dependencies,
   but testing interactions often involves verifying
   if a mocked method was called with a particular
   argument. *Arg.Is* is typically used in NSubstitute
   to match the arguments passed to a method.
   ExpectedObjects makes this even more powerful
   because it allows you to easily match complex
   objects passed to a mocked method by comparing
   them to an expected object.

Let's put it in practice. Listing 3-16 demonstrates the *EmployeeService*
class, which implements the *GetByIdAsync* method. This method returns
an *Employee* object (which inherits from the *User* class), as shown in
Listing 3-17. The *User* object returned by the *GetByIdAsync* method of
the *IUserRepository* interface is mapped onto an *Employee* object, which
is then returned as an output parameter. Before being returned, the
Employee object is passed as a parameter to the *LogAsync* method of the
ILogAccessService interface, as shown in Listing 3-18.

Listing 3-16. The EmployeeService class

```
using Apress.UnitTests.Interfaces;
using Apress.UnitTests.Models;

namespace Apress.UnitTests.Services;

public class EmployeeService
{
    private readonly IUserRepository _userRepository;
    private readonly ILogAccessService _logService;

    public EmployeeService(IUserRepository userRepository,
    ILogAccessService logService)
    {
        _userRepository = userRepository;
        _logService = logService;
    }

    public async Task<Employee> GetByIdAsync(int id)
    {
        var user = await _userRepository.GetByIdAsync(id);

        if (user is null)
            return null;
        else
        {
            var employee = new Employee
            {
                Id = user.Id,
                FirstName = user.FirstName,
                LastName = user.LastName,
                Email = user.Email,
                IsActive = user.IsActive,
```

```
              CompanyName = "MyCompany"
        };
        await _logService.LogAsync(employee);
        return employee;
    }
  }
}
```

Listing 3-17. The Employee class

```
namespace Apress.UnitTests.Models;

public class Employee : User
{
    public string CompanyName { get; set; }
}
```

Listing 3-18. The ILogAccessService interface

```
using Apress.UnitTests.Models;

namespace Apress.UnitTests.Interfaces;

public interface ILogAccessService
{
    Task LogAsync(Employee person);
}
```

Now let's unit test it! Listing 3-19 shows the *EmployeeServiceTests* class that implements the *GetByIdAsync_WhenGetByIdAsyncReturn ANonNullUser_ShouldReturnAnEmployeeObjectCorrectlyFilled AndInvokeLogAsync* test method. This unit test verifies that when *GetByIdAsync* returns a non-null *User*, it correctly maps the User to an *Employee* object. It then checks that the *Employee* object is correctly filled with data and that the *LogAsync* method is called once with the correct *Employee* object. The test ensures both proper data mapping and logging behavior.

Listing 3-19. The EmployeeServiceTests class

```
using Apress.UnitTests.Interfaces;
using Apress.UnitTests.Models;
using Apress.UnitTests.Services;
using AutoFixture;
using ExpectedObjects;
using FluentAssertions;
using NSubstitute;
using Xunit;

namespace Apress.UnitTests;

public class EmployeeServiceTests
{
    private readonly Fixture _fixture;
    private readonly IUserRepository _userRepositoryMock;
    private readonly ILogAccessService _logAccessServiceMock;
    private readonly EmployeeService _sut;

    public EmployeeServiceTests()
    {
        _fixture = new Fixture();
        _userRepositoryMock = Substitute.For<IUserRepository>();
        _logAccessServiceMock = Substitute.For<ILogAccess
        Service>();
        _sut = new EmployeeService(_userRepositoryMock, _log
        AccessServiceMock);
    }
```

```
[Fact]
public async Task GetByIdAsync_WhenGetByIdAsyncReturn
ANonNullUser_ShouldReturnAnEmployeeObjectCorrectlyFilled
AndInvokeLogAsync()
    {
        // Arrange
        var id = _fixture.Create<int>();
        var user = _fixture.Create<User>();
        _userRepositoryMock.GetByIdAsync(Arg.Any<int>()).
        Returns(user);
        var expectedEmployee = new Employee
        {
            Id = user.Id,
            FirstName = user.FirstName,
            LastName = user.LastName,
            Email = user.Email,
            IsActive = user.IsActive,
            CompanyName = "MyCompany"
        }.ToExpectedObject();

        // Act
        var employee = await _sut.GetByIdAsync(id);

        // Assert
        expectedEmployee.Equals(employee);
        await _logAccessServiceMock.Received(1).LogAsync
        (Arg.Is<Employee>(emp => expectedEmployee.
        Equals(emp)));
    }
}
```

As you can see, ExpectedObjects helps simplify and improve object comparisons by automatically performing a deep equality check on the entire structure of the *Employee* object, including all its properties like *Id*, *FirstName*, *LastName*, etc. This eliminates the need for manually checking each individual property, making the assertion more concise and readable. The *Equals* method of ExpectedObjects is used to verify that the actual *Employee* object returned by *GetByIdAsync* matches the expected one, streamlining the comparison process; the same *Equals* method is also combined with NSubstitute and evaluates the *Employee* object passed to the *LogAsync* method. By using ExpectedObjects, the test ensures accuracy in the comparison, reducing the chance of missing subtle differences in object structure. If new properties are added or existing ones change, the test continues to function correctly without needing updates to the assertion logic. This makes ExpectedObjects a reliable tool for verifying that the actual *Employee* object matches the expected one, including nested properties, without having to write out comparisons for each individual field explicitly.

Earlier in this chapter, I opted to use classes instead of Structs or Records because I wanted to demonstrate how to validate class instances as parameters (including output parameters). The ExpectedObjects library helps verify whether an instance matches property values rather than just the reference. Therefore, if you are working with Structs or Records, you won't need to use ExpectedObjects.

To finish, I'd like to warn you about ExpectedObjects: it has some limitations, like struggling with verifying:

- **Circular References, Nested Collections**: When working with deeply nested collections or complex object graphs, ExpectedObjects can become cumbersome and may require custom handling. It doesn't automatically support verifying deep object hierarchies or handling nested collections with fine-grained control.

- **Dynamic Objects**: Example: var obj = { Property1 = "Value1" }

- **Stream Objects**: Like *Stream, FileStream, NetworkStream,* etc.

For these scenarios, I suggest you not to use ExpectedObjects, or else your test will crash.

However, there is a solution. You can test the properties one by one. The *Arg.Is<T>* argument allows you to customize the test for your parameter. It is possible to generate a condition in the form of a lambda expression as a parameter of *Arg.Is<T>*, and it is done as follows if we refer to the assertion in Listing 3-19:

```
await _logAccessServiceMock.Received(1).LogAsync(Arg.
Is<Employee>(emp => emp.Id == expectedEmployee.Id &&
emp.FirstName == expectedEmployee.FirstName &&
emp.LastName == expectedEmployee.LastName &&
emp.Email == expectedEmployee.Email &&
emp.IsActive == expectedEmployee.IsActive &&
emp.CompanyName == expectedEmployee.CompanyName));
```

If you have many properties, it may take a long time to write, but it can save you. In any case, you are not required to use ExpectedObjects, even though you are not limited in its use. I know people who prefer to test the properties one by one, and that works just fine, too!

Running Your First Unit Test

You have two options for running your unit tests: you can either use Test Explorer in Visual Studio or run them via the command prompt or terminal using the .NET *CLI (Command Line Interface)*, depending on your preference. Both options require the installation of the NuGet packages as described earlier in the chapter.

Using Visual Studio

Step 1: Open Test Explorer

Go to **Test ➤ Test Explorer** to open the **Test Explorer** window. This panel
will display all of your unit tests. Figure 3-3 shows **Test Explorer** on the top
panel of Visual Studio, and Figure 3-4 shows **Test Explorer** opened.

Figure 3-3. *The Test Explorer panel of Visual Studio*

Figure 3-4. *Test Explorer opened in Visual Studio*

Step 2: Run the Tests

In Visual Studio you can run all the tests in the project; click the **Run All** button in the **Test Explorer** window (a green triangle). You also can run a specific test; find the test in the **Test Explorer** window, right-click it, and select **Run**. Figure 3-5 shows the Run All button on the top left and the individual test to get in the panel.

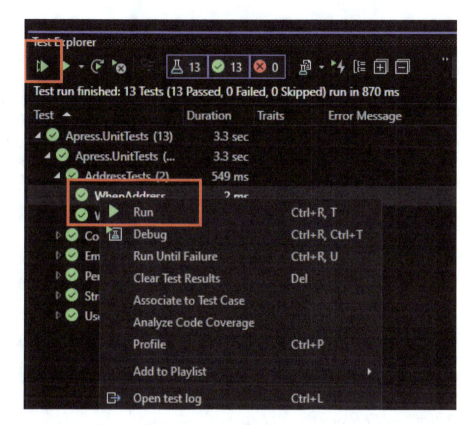

Figure 3-5. *Run the tests in Visual Studio*

Step 3: Check Test Results

After running the tests, the **Test Explorer** window will update to show the results of the test run. Green icons indicate successful tests, and red icons show failed tests. If a test fails, you can click the test in **Test Explorer** to view detailed output and stack trace to help you diagnose the issue. Figure 3-6 shows the results of successful unit test execution.

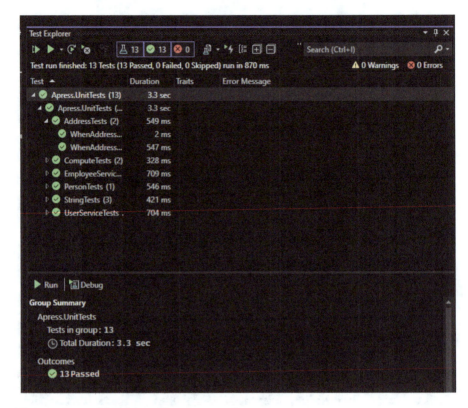

Figure 3-6. *Checking the test results*

Using the CLI

Step 1: Open the Command Line or Terminal

Open a terminal or command prompt on your system. For Windows, you can use **Command Prompt** or **PowerShell**, and for macOS/Linux, you can use your terminal.

Step 2: Navigate to Your Test Project

Use the cd (change directory) command to navigate to the directory containing your test project; for example, on my computer, it gives the following:

```
cd C:\Users\antho\source\repos\Apress\UnitTestCookBook
```

Step 3: Restore Your Dependencies (If Necessary)

If you haven't already restored the project dependencies (e.g., NuGet packages), run the following command:

```
dotnet restore
```

This will restore the required packages specified in your project files.

Step 4: Build the Test Project

Before running the tests, you can build the project using

```
dotnet build
```

Step 5: Run the Tests

Run the following command that will discover and run all the tests:

```
dotnet test
```

If you want to run a specific unit test project, provide the path of the csproj project as follows:

```
dotnet test {fullpath}\UnitTestCookBookApress.UnitTests.csproj
```

Step 6: Check the Results

After completing the execution of the tests, the output should look like Figure 3-7, with the number of tests passed, failed, or skipped and the duration.

```
C:\Users\antho\source\repos\Apress\UnitTestCookBook> dotnet test C:\Users\antho\source\repos\Apress\UnitTestCookBook\Apr
ess.UnitTests.csproj
Restore complete (0.3s)
  Apress.UnitTests succeeded (0.2s) → bin\Debug\net9.0\Apress.UnitTests.dll
[xUnit.net 00:00:00.00] xUnit.net VSTest Adapter v3.0.2+dd36e86129 (64-bit .NET 9.0.2)
[xUnit.net 00:00:00.08]   Discovering: Apress.UnitTests
[xUnit.net 00:00:00.12]   Discovered:  Apress.UnitTests
[xUnit.net 00:00:00.14]   Starting:    Apress.UnitTests
[xUnit.net 00:00:00.27]   Finished:    Apress.UnitTests
  Apress.UnitTests test succeeded (0.9s)

Test summary: total: 13, failed: 0, succeeded: 13, skipped: 0, duration: 0.9s
Build succeeded in 2.0s
C:\Users\antho\source\repos\Apress\UnitTestCookBook> |
```

Figure 3-7. *The test execution output in the terminal*

Summary

In this chapter, you have learned how to write effective unit tests using xUnit, NSubstitute, FluentAssertions, AutoFixture, and ExpectedObjects. Use AutoFixture to automatically generate test data, reducing the need for manual setup. Mock dependencies with NSubstitute to control the behavior of external services or repositories (and their parameters). Write assertions with FluentAssertions for more readable and expressive checks, avoiding traditional Assert statements. Use ExpectedObjects to compare complex objects, ensuring deep equality checks without manually comparing individual properties. Finally, ensure that tests are focused, independent, and maintainable so they remain clear and easy to update as the implementation evolves. You have also learned how to run your unit tests on your machine. You are good to go! In the next chapter, we will explore the most common challenges encountered when unit testing .NET applications.

CHAPTER 4

Unit Test .NET Applications

In the previous chapters, we explored best practices for writing effective and reliable unit tests, focusing on techniques to ensure tests are maintainable and readable. Building on this foundation, this chapter will concentrate on particular cases encountered when writing unit tests for .NET applications. We will examine some challenges. In this chapter, we will see how to handle the following situations:

- Dealing with DataTable

- Dealing with DateTime

- Dealing with extension methods

- Dealing with private classes/methods

- Dealing with internal classes

- Dealing with abstract classes and virtual methods

- Dealing with HttpClient

- Dealing with infrastructure components

© Anthony Giretti 2025
A. Giretti, *The Unit Testing Practice Cookbook*,
https://doi.org/10.1007/979-8-8688-1454-9_4

Dealing with DataTables

In some applications, *DataTables* are used instead of strongly typed objects due to their flexibility, compatibility with legacy systems, and ability to handle dynamic or schema-less data structures. *DataTables* are part of the ADO.NET framework and are designed to represent in-memory, tabular data structures, making them convenient when working with relational databases or structured query results. Many legacy .NET applications and libraries are built around ADO.NET, which natively uses *DataTables*. Migrating to strongly typed objects could require significant refactoring. In this section, I'll show you how to unit test easily a service where the repository returns a *DataTable*.

Let's consider a repository named *IOrderRepository* that exposes a method named *GetAsync*, which returns a *DataTable* of three columns:

1. Id (long)

2. Amount (decimal)

3. Date (DateTime)

The *OrderService* class will implement a method called *GetAsync* that will return a list of *Order* objects, and we want to unit test that mapping. Listing 4-1 shows the *Order* class, Listing 4-2 the *IOrderRepository* interface, and Listing 4-3 the *OrderService* class.

Listing 4-1. The Order class

```
namespace Apress.UnitTests.DataTables;

public class Order
{
    public long Id { get; set; }
    public decimal Amount { get; set; }
    public DateTime Date { get; set; }
}
```

Listing 4-2. The IOrderRepository interface

```
using System.Data;

namespace Apress.UnitTests.DataTables;

public interface IOrderRepository
{
    Task<DataTable> GetAsync();
}
```

Listing 4-3. The OrderService class

```
using System.Data;

namespace Apress.UnitTests.DataTables;

public class OrderService
{
    private readonly IOrderRepository _orderRepository;

    public OrderService(IOrderRepository orderRepository)
    {
        _orderRepository = orderRepository;
    }

    public async Task<List<Order>> GetAsync()
    {
        var table = await _orderRepository.GetAsync();
        var orders = new List<Order>();

        foreach (DataRow row in table.Rows)
        {
            var order = new Order
            {
                Id = row.Field<long>("Id"),
```

```
                Amount = row.Field<decimal>("Amount"),
                Date = row.Field<DateTime>("Date")
            };

            orders.Add(order);
        }
        return orders;
    }
}
```

The code is pretty simple, but unit testing is more complex because we have created a mockup of the *DataTable* that will be mapped to a list of *Order* objects.

Setting up a *DataTable* is pretty long; unfortunately, AutoFixture does not handle it. The following code snippet shows how to set the *DataTable* mentioned earlier with three rows:

```
DataTable table = new DataTable("MyTable");
DataColumn idColumn = new DataColumn("id", typeof(int));
DataColumn amountColumn = new DataColumn("amount",
typeof(decimal));
DataColumn dateColumn = new DataColumn("date",
typeof(DateTime));
table.Columns.Add(idColumn);
table.Columns.Add(amountColumn);
table.Columns.Add(dateColumn);
DataRow newRow = table.NewRow();
newRow["id"] = 1;
newRow["amount"] = 10.3m;
newRow["date"] = new DateTime(2018, 10, 20);
table.Rows.Add(newRow);
newRow = table.NewRow();
```

```
newRow["id"] = 2;
newRow["amount"] = 42.1m;
newRow["date"] = new DateTime(2018, 04, 12);
table.Rows.Add(newRow);
newRow = table.NewRow();
newRow["id"] = 2;
newRow["amount"] = 5.6;
newRow["date"] = new DateTime(2018, 07, 2);
table.Rows.Add(newRow);
```

As you can see, it's not handy, and it's only about filling three rows of three columns. We certainly don't want that in our unit test Arrange phase! To simplify it, I will show you how to use the Newtonsoft.Json library to transform a JSON file into a DataTable easily! Much readable it will be!

Note   Newtonsoft.Json is a popular high-performance JSON framework for .NET. It is widely used for serializing (converting .NET objects to JSON) and deserializing (converting JSON to .NET objects) data.

System.Text.Json, another JSON framework that is commonly used in newer versions of .NET and tends to replace Newtonsoft.Json, does not support the JSON transformation into DataTables.

Dealing with money requires being careful in C# and Newtonsoft. Json. By default, this library reads *decimal* types as *double* types, so we will need to tweak the *Order* class, its *Amount* property especially. We will need to write a custom serialization for decimal types, represented by the *DecimalJsonConverter* class as shown in Listing 4-4.

Listing 4-4. The DecimalJsonConverter class

```
using System.Text.Json;
using System.Text.Json.Serialization;

namespace Apress.UnitTests.DataTables.Helpers;

public class DecimalJsonConverter : JsonConverter<decimal>
{
    public override decimal Read(ref Utf8JsonReader reader,
    Type typeToConvert, JsonSerializerOptions options)
    {
        return reader.GetDecimal();
    }

    public override void Write(Utf8JsonWriter writer, decimal
    value, JsonSerializerOptions options)
    {
        writer.WriteNumberValue(value);
    }
}
```

Once coded, let's apply it as an attribute on the *Amount* property of the *Order* class as shown in Listing 4-5.

Listing 4-5. The Order class

```
using Apress.UnitTests.DataTables.Helpers;
using System.Text.Json.Serialization;

namespace Apress.UnitTests.DataTables;

public class Order
{
    public long Id { get; set; }
    [JsonConverter(typeof(DecimalJsonConverter))]
```

```
    public decimal Amount { get; set; }
    public DateTime Date { get; set; }
}
```

Now, let's create the JSON containing the data to be mapped into a *DataTable* for our unit test. Listing 4-6 shows the JSON file, named datatable.json, that contains fake data for testing purposes.

Listing 4-6. The datatable.json file

```
[
  {
    "id": 1,
    "amount": "10,3",
    "date": "2025-01-20T00:00:00"
  },
  {
    "id": 2,
    "amount": "42.1",
    "date": "2025-02-12T00:00:00"
  },
  {
    "id": 3,
    "amount": "5.6",
    "date": "2025-02-02T00:00:00"
  }
]
```

This file must be included in your unit test project and be declared as an "Embedded resource" for the **Build Action** directive and set to "Copy always" for the **Copy to Output Directory** directive as shown in Figure 4-1.

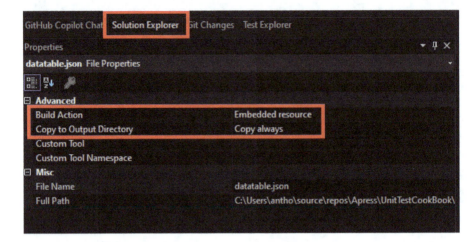

Figure 4-1. *The datatable.json file Build Action and Copy to Output Directory directives*

We need now to write a little helper in C#, named *EmbeddedJsonFileHelper,* based on Newtonsoft.Json to read the file and fill a *DataTable* as shown in Listing 4-7.

Listing 4-7. The EmbeddedJsonFileHelper class

```csharp
using Newtonsoft.Json;

namespace Apress.UnitTests.DataTables.Helpers;

public static class EmbeddedJsonFileHelper
{
    public static T GetContent<T>(string filename)
    {
        return JsonConvert.DeserializeObject<T>(File.ReadAll
        Text($"{filename}.json"));
    }
}
```

We are ready to write our unit test! Listing 4-8 shows the *Order ServiceTests* test class with its test method named *GetAsync_WhenGet AsyncRepositoryMethodReturnAFilledDataTable_GetAsyncServiceMethod ReturnsAListOfTransactions.*

Listing 4-8. The OrderServiceTests class

```
using Apress.UnitTests.DataTables;
using Apress.UnitTests.DataTables.Helpers;
using ExpectedObjects;
using NSubstitute;
using System.Data;
using Xunit;

namespace Apress.UnitTests;

public class OrderServiceTests
{
    [Fact]
    public async Task GetAsync_WhenGetAsyncRepository
    MethodReturnAFilledDataTable_GetAsyncServiceMethod
    ReturnsAListOfTransactions()
    {
        // Arrange
        IOrderRepository orderRepositoryMock =    Substitute.
        For<IOrderRepository>();
        DataTable table = new DataTable();
        table.Columns.Add("Id", typeof(long));
        table.Columns.Add("Quantity", typeof(int));
        table.Columns.Add("Date", typeof(DateTime));

        var datatable = EmbeddedJsonFileHelper.GetContent
        <DataTable>(@"DataTables\datatable");
        foreach (DataRow row in datatable.Rows)
```

```
        {
            table.ImportRow(row);
        }

        orderRepositoryMock.GetAsync().Returns(x => table);
        var expectedResult = new List<Order>
        {
            new Order { Id = 1, Quantity = 10, Date = DateTime.
            Parse("2025-01-20") },
            new Order { Id = 2, Quantity = 20, Date = DateTime.
            Parse("2025-02-12")},
            new Order { Id = 3, Quantity = 30, Date = DateTime.
            Parse("2025-02-02")}
    }.ToExpectedObject();

        // Act
        var service = new OrderService(orderRepositoryMock);
        var result = await service.GetAsync();

        // Assert
        expectedResult.ShouldEqual(result);
    }
}
```

As you can see, I have reused the libraries I introduced in the previous chapter. Additionally, using JSON to mock a *DataTable* greatly improved the test efficiency and readability! However, I had to create a DataTable manually with only the columns. Why? When using Newtonsoft.Json to deserialize JSON into a *DataTable*, integer numbers are often converted into long instead of int. This behavior occurs because Newtonsoft.Json uses the most inclusive numeric type (long) by default to avoid data loss from large numbers. Same for decimal, it's using doubles instead of decimal. That's why I mapped the DataTable created by Newtonsoft.Json to a newer one, which has the proper types. It's not perfect, but it's definitely better than manually arranging too many lines of data!

All those tips made this unit test extremely simple!

I hope you liked this tip. 😊

Dealing with DateTimes

You have worked on many projects (and probably all of them) utilizing *DateTimes*. In my career, this was the case, and 100% of the time, I used *DateTimes*, especially with how *DateTime.Now* or *DateTime.Utc* caused such a challenge for unit testing. Why? Because it's difficult to unit test methods that use *DateTime.Now* (or *UtcNow*) directly because *DateTime. Now/UtcNow* is a static, system-dependent, and non-deterministic property. It always returns the current system time, which constantly changes, making tests unpredictable, flaky, and non-repeatable. In this section, I will show you how to refactor your code to unit test a method with the current time. Listing 4-9 shows the DateUtilities class that implements a method named *IsAfternoon*. This method returns, by using the current time, if the current time is part of the afternoon by returning True or False.

Listing 4-9. The DateUtilities class

```
namespace Apress.UnitTests.DateTimes;

public class DateUtilities
{
    public DateUtilities() { }

    public bool IsAfternoon()
```

```
    {
        return DateTime.Now.Hour > 12;
    }
}
```

As I mentioned earlier, if we perform a unit test, it will not work consistently, depending on the time of day. To effectively test this logic, we will need to mock *DateTime.Now*. How? By injecting a *DateTime* provider into the constructor.

In .NET 7 and earlier versions, we will use *ISystemClock*.

In .NET 8 and later versions, we will use *TimeProvider*.

Note *ISystemClock* is part of the Microsoft.Extensions.Internal namespace, which can be acquired from the Microsoft.Extensions. Caching.Abstractions NuGet package.

They are not utilizable as is; you'll need to register them into the Dependency Injection container, as shown in the following code snippet:

```
var builder = WebApplication.CreateApplication.
CreateBuilder(TimeProvider.System);
builder.Services.AddSingleton<TimeProvider>(TimeProvider.
System); // TimeProvider
builder.Services.AddSingleton<ISystemClock, SystemClock>();
// ISystemClock
```

Listings 4-10 and 4-11, respectively, show both providers implemented in the refactored *DateUtilities* class.

Listing 4-10. The DateUtilities class refactored with ISystemClock

```
using Microsoft.Extensions.Internal;

namespace Apress.UnitTests.DateTimes;

public class DateUtilities
{
    private readonly ISystemClock _systemClock;
    public DateUtilities(ISystemClock systemClock)
    {
        _systemClock = systemClock;
    }

    public bool IsAfternoon()
    {
        return _systemClock.UtcNow.LocalDateTime.Hour > 12;
    }
}
```

Listing 4-11. The DateUtilities class refactored with TimeProvider

```
public class DateUtilities
{
    private readonly TimeProvider _timeProvider;
    public DateUtilities(TimeProvider timeProvider)
    {
        _timeProvider = timeProvider;
    }

    public bool IsAfternoon()
    {
        return _timeProvider.GetLocalNow().Hour > 12;
    }
}
```

Listings 4-12 and 4-13 show, respectively, how to unit test them.

Listing 4-12. The DateUtilitiesTests test class with ISystemClock

```
using AutoFixture;
using FluentAssertions;
using Microsoft.Extensions.Internal;
using NSubstitute;
using Xunit;

namespace Apress.UnitTests.DateTimes;

public class DateUtilitiesTests
{
    [Fact]
    public void IsAfternoon_WhenCurrentDateTimeIsBefore
    Noon_ShouldReturnFalse()
    {
        // Arrange
        var systemClockMock = Substitute.For<ISystemClock>();
        var fixture = new Fixture();
        fixture.Customizations.Add(new RandomNumericSequence
        Generator(0, 11));
        var hour = fixture.Create<int>();
        var mockTime = new DateTimeOffset(new DateTime(2025, 2,
        17, hour, 0, 0));
        systemClockMock.UtcNow.Returns(mockTime);
        var sut = new DateUtilities1(systemClockMock);

        // Act
        var result = sut.IsAfternoon();
```

```
    // Assert
    result.Should().BeFalse();
  }
}
```

When mocking *ISystemClock*, I had to create a substitute for it, but I also needed to set up a *DateTimeOffset* from the mocked *DateTime*. As you can see, I'm using *the UtcNow property*, but don't worry, since I'm mocking *DateTimeOffset*, the latter will automatically capture the local time (with the system's local offset) from the *DateTime* passed as a parameter. The test will utilize the local time, and the test will pass.

Listing 4-13. The DateUtilities test class with TimeProvider

```
[Fact]
public void IsAfternoon_WhenCurrentDateTimeIsBeforeNoon_Should
ReturnFalse()
{
    // Arrange
    var fakeTimeProvider = new FakeTimeProvider();
    var hour = _fixture.Create<int>();
    var mockTime = new DateTimeOffset(new DateTime(2025, 2, 17,
    hour, 0, 0));
    fakeTimeProvider.SetUtcNow(new DateTimeOffset(new
    DateTime(2025, 2, 17, hour, 0, 0)));
    var sut = new DateUtilities2(fakeTimeProvider);

    // Act
    var result = sut.IsAfternoon();

    // Assert
    result.Should().BeFalse();
}
```

Testing *TimeProvider* is slightly different. Mocking *TimeProvider* with NSubstitute (or any other mocking library) will not work because it won't mock the *TimeZoneInfo* internally, which is necessary to invoke the *GetLocalNow* method. To overcome that, Microsoft has released a NuGet package you can download as follows:

```
NuGet\Install-Package Microsoft.Extensions.TimeProvider.Testing
```

From this, I used the *FakeTimeProvider* class fed with the DateTimeOffset class. Like *ISystemClock*, the local datetime will be captured even though I'm setting the date using the *SetUtcNow* method. The rest of the test is similar to *ISystemClock*.

These examples represent best practices for handling *DateTime* in your code. I strongly recommend refactoring your code if it doesn't adhere to these practices; otherwise, unit testing will be difficult or impossible.

Dealing with Extension Methods

Extension methods in C# are **static methods** that act as if they are part of an existing type but are defined in a separate static class. While they enhance code readability and maintainability, they introduce challenges in **unit testing**, particularly when using mocking libraries like **NSubstitute**. Since extension methods are just **static methods in disguise**, they cannot be overridden in derived classes or mocked like instance methods.

Common Challenges with Extension Methods

To describe the challenge with extension methods, let's use some examples I have shown you in the previous chapter, like the *UserService* class. Let's modify it to add a method named *GetUserName* that returns a string. The *GetUserName* method will invoke the *IUserRepository* and return the username of the user based on their *FirstName* and their *LastName*.

This logic is defined on an extension method also named *GetUserName* and part of the *UserExtensions* static class. Listing 4-14 shows the *UserExtensions* class, and Listing 4-15 shows the *UserService* class.

Listing 4-14. The UserExtensions class

```
namespace Apress.UnitTests.ExtensionMethods;

public static class UserExtensions
{
    public static string GetUserName(this User user)
    {
        if (user == null)
            return null;
        return $"{user.FirstName}{user.FirstName}";
    }
}
```

Listing 4-15. The UserService class

```
namespace Apress.UnitTests.ExtensionMethods;

public class UserService
{
    private readonly IUserRepository _userRepository;

    public UserService(IUserRepository userRepository)
    {
        _userRepository = userRepository;
    }

    public async Task<string> GetUserName(int id)
    {
        if (id > 0)
```

```
            return (await _userRepository.GetByIdAsync(id)).
            GetUserName();
        return await Task.FromResult<string>(null);
    }
}
```

As you can see here, when unit testing the *GetUserName* method of the *UserService* class, you will have to unit test the *GetUserName* extension method **at the same time** because it cannot be mocked, as it is a concrete implementation and not an interface. This is not ideal because you will mix the extension method's behavior with the *UserService* behavior:

1.   Testing GetUserName when id is lower than 0

2.   Testing GetUserName when id is greater than 0 and when User is null

3.   Testing GetUserName when id is greater than 0 and when User is not null but FirstName is null or empty

4.   Testing GetUserName when id is greater than 0 and when User is not null but LastName is null or empty

5.   Testing GetUserName when id is greater than 0 and when User is not null but FirstName and LastName are null or empty

In that case, you must realize the consequences of how *UserService* is implemented (through an extension method where the mapping of *User's* *FirstName* and *LastName* returns a username).

To avoid that and not complexify the unit test, the best practice is to turn the extension method into an injectable service through an interface. Listing 4-16 shows the *UserUtilityService* and its related interface *IUserUtilityService*.

Listing 4-16. The UserUtilityService class and the
IUserUtilityService interface

```
namespace Apress.UnitTests.ExtensionMethods;

public interface IUserUtilityService
{
    string GetUserName(User user);
}

public class UserUtilityService : IUserUtilityService
{
    public string GetUserName(User user)
    {
        if (user == null)
            return null;
        return $"{user.FirstName}{user.FirstName}";
    }
}
```

And now let's rewrite the *UserService* class as shown in Listing 4-17.

Listing 4-17. The rewritten UserService class

```
namespace Apress.UnitTests.ExtensionMethods;

public class UserService
{
    private readonly IUserRepository _userRepository;
    private readonly IUserUtilityService _userUtilityService;

    public UserService(IUserRepository userRepository,
                       IUserUtilityService userUtilityService)
    {
        _userRepository = userRepository;
```

```
        _userUtilityService= userUtilityService;
    }
    public async Task<string> GetUserName(int id)
    {
        if (id > 0)
            return _userUtilityService.GetUserName(await _user
            Repository.GetByIdAsync(id));
        return await Task.FromResult<string>(null);
    }
}
```

Now, let me be clear—if you occasionally use extension methods, as I just demonstrated, it's not a big deal. However, if you overuse them, then, yes, it will become a problem for your unit tests.

The takeaway is that you should think carefully about this topic. This doesn't mean you should **never** use extension methods, but rather that you should use them wisely.

The Challenge with ILogger

ILogger is hard to unit test primarily because logging methods (e.g., *LogInformation*, *LogError*, etc.) are extension methods, meaning they cannot be directly mocked or intercepted. Here's why:

1. **They Bypass Virtual Methods**: Since LogInformation(), LogError(), etc. are extension methods, they do not belong to ILogger<T> directly but are wrappers around ILogger.Log(). Mocking frameworks like NSubstitute cannot override extension methods.

2. **You Must Verify the Underlying *Log()***
   Method: Instead of verifying *logger.
   LogInformation("message")*, you must verify *logger.
   Log(LogLevel.Information, ...)* with the correct
   parameters.

Listing 4-18 shows the *AuthenticationService*, which does nothing
except invoke *ILogger* for simplicity.

Listing 4-18. The AuthenticationService class

```
using Microsoft.Extensions.Logging;

namespace Apress.UnitTests.ExtensionMethods;

public class AuthenticationService
{
    private readonly ILogger<AuthService> _logger;

    public AuthService(ILogger<AuthService> logger)
    {
        _logger = logger;
    }

    public void Login(string userId)
    {
        _logger.LogInformation("User {UserId} has logged in",
        userId);
    }
}
```

What does the unit test look like? Listing 4-19 shows it.

Listing 4-19. The AuthenticationServiceTests class

```
using AutoFixture;
using Microsoft.Extensions.Logging;
using NSubstitute;
using Xunit;

namespace Apress.UnitTests.ExtensionMethods;

public class AuthenticationServiceTests
{
    [Fact]
    public void Login_WhenLoginIsInvoked_Should_InvokeLogger
    WithCorrectParameters()
    {
        // Arrange
        var fixture = new Fixture();
        var logger = Substitute.For<ILogger<AuthService>>();
        var authService = new AuthService(logger);
        var userId = fixture.Create<string>();

        // Act
        authService.Login(userId);

        // Assert
        logger.Received(1).Log(
            LogLevel.Information,
            // Ensure it's an Information log
            Arg.Any<EventId>(),                // Ignore EventId
            Arg.Is<object>(o =>
                o.ToString().Equals($"User {userId} has logged in")
                // Ensure correct message template and its
                parameters
            ),
```

```
            Arg.Any<Exception>(),
            // Ignore exceptions
            Arg.Any<Func<object, Exception, string>>()
            // Ignore formatter
        );
    }
}
```

As you can see, the internal Log method of *ILogger* includes several parameters, such as *EventId*, *Exception*, and the *Formatter* delegate, which can be ignored. Since testing them is both unnecessary and complex, we will focus solely on the *LogLevel* and the message template (and its parameters, if any). So you understand that unit testing a service with *ILogger* is neither straightforward nor elegant. But don't worry, there is a solution, and I'm pretty sure you will like it!

For unit testing purposes, Microsoft has released a NuGet package, and you can download it as follows:

```
NuGet\Install-Package Microsoft.Extensions.
Diagnostics.Testing
```

Note   *FakeLogger* is only available since .NET 8. So, if you are still using an earlier version of .NET, I suggest upgrading to .NET 8 or later or using the solution I showed you earlier.

This package provides the *FakeLogger* class that allows you to mock the *ILogger*. Listing 4-20 shows the preceding unit test reworked with *FakeLogger*.

Listing 4-20. The AuthenticationServiceTests class refactored with
the FakeLogger class

```
using AutoFixture;
using FluentAssertions;
using Microsoft.Extensions.Logging;
using Microsoft.Extensions.Logging.Testing;
using NSubstitute;
using Xunit;

namespace Apress.UnitTests.ExtensionMethods;

public class AuthServiceTests
{
    [Fact]
    public void Login_WhenLoginIsInvoked_Should_InvokeLogger
    WithCorrectParameters_FakeLogger()
    {
        // Arrange
        var fixture = new Fixture();
        var logger = new FakeLogger<AuthService>();
        var authService = new AuthService(logger);
        var userId = fixture.Create<string>();

        // Act
        authService.Login(userId);

        // Assert
        logger.Collector.LatestRecord.Level.Should().Be
        (LogLevel.Information);
        logger.Collector.LatestRecord.Message.Should().Be
        ($"User {userId} has logged in");
    }
}
```

It's much more straightforward, can't you see? *FakeLogger* provides two essential properties that greatly simplify *ILogger* testing:

1. **Collector**: This property allows you to view all log messages gathered during your tests. You can retrieve and analyze these logs to gain insights into the test execution process.

2. **LatestRecord**: This property provides access to the last log message captured during testing.

Isn't that great? I strongly suggest you use *FakeLogger* if you want to verify your log when unit testing a method.

Dealing with Private Methods

A codebase often contains many private methods in cases where a class has complex internal logic broken down into smaller helper methods for readability and reusability. This typically happens in

1. **Business Logic Services**: Complex business may include private methods for validation and calculations.

2. **Legacy Code**: Old, monolithic classes often contain many private methods due to insufficient refactoring.

Unit testing private methods or classes is generally considered a **bad practice** because it **breaks encapsulation** and tightly coupled tests to implementation details, making refactoring harder. Private methods could be tested **indirectly** through public methods that use them (if the private method is too complex, it will also make the public method test complex). Generally, it's better to refactor it in a separate, testable, and ideally injectable by dependency; the reasoning is the same as the extension methods we discussed earlier. However, you may want to unit test private methods anyway, for some reason that belongs to you, and I will show you how to make it. Listing 4-21 shows the *User* class containing the *ValidateAndGetUserName* method, which uses the *GetUserName* private method internally.

Listing 4-21. The User class

```
namespace Apress.UnitTests.PrivateMethods;

public class User
{
    private string _firstName { get; set; }
    private string _lastName { get; set; }

    public User(string firstName, string lastName)
    {
        _firstName = firstName;
        _lastName = lastName;
    }

    public string ValidateAndGetUserName()
    {
        if (string.IsNullOrWhiteSpace(_firstName) || string.
        IsNullOrWhiteSpace(_firstName))
            throw new Exception("Data is missing !");

        return this.GetUserName(_firstName, _lastName);
    }

    private string GetUserName(string firstName, string
    lastName) => $"{firstName} {lastName} !";
}
```

As you may know, in C#, private methods and classes are not directly accessible for unit testing. The solution here is to use reflection. Listing 4-22 shows the *UserTests* class unit testing the *User* class and particularly its *GetUserName* method.

Listing 4-22. The UserTests class

```
using AutoFixture;
using FluentAssertions;
using System.Reflection;
using Xunit;

namespace Apress.UnitTests.PrivateMethods;

public class UserTests
{
    [Fact]
    public void GetUserName_WhenGetUserNameIsInvoked_Should
    ReturnUserNameProperly()
    {
        // Arrange
        var fixture = new Fixture();
        var firstname = fixture.Create<string>();
        var lastname = fixture.Create<string>();

        Type type = typeof(User);
        var user = Activator.CreateInstance(type, firstname,
        lastname);
        MethodInfo method = type.GetMethods(BindingFlags.
        NonPublic | BindingFlags.Instance)
        .Where(x => x.Name == "GetUserName" && x.IsPrivate)
        .First();
```

```
        //Act
        var getUserName = (string)method.Invoke(user, null);

        //Assert
        getUserName
        .Should()
        .Be($"{firstname} {lastname}");
    }
}
```

This test utilizes AutoFixture, FluentAssertions, and xUnit as usual, and I won't explain it again here. However, four steps involve reflection that needs to be explained:

1. **Creating a *User Type* Variable**:

   - The *typeof(User)* expression creates an object of type *Type*, which is essential for performing reflection operations on the *User* class.

   - A *Type* object holds all metadata about the *User* type, allowing further inspection and manipulation.

2. **Dynamically Creating a User Instance**:

   - The *Activator.CreateInstance* method is used to instantiate an object of the User class dynamically.

   - It takes *firstname* and *lastname* as parameters, assuming they match the constructor of the *User* class.

3. **Retrieving the Private Method**:

   - The *GetMethods* method allows searching for methods within the *User* type.

- By applying *BindingFlags.NonPublic | BindingFlags. Instance*, the search is restricted to private instance methods.

- The test locates the private *GetUserName* method and stores it in a *MethodInfo* object, enabling access to the method for testing.

4. **Invoking the Private Method**:

- Using the *MethodInfo.Invoke* method, the test executes the *GetUserName* method on the dynamically created *User* instance.

- The first parameter is the *User* object on which the method is invoked.

- The second parameter is *null*, indicating that *GetUserName* does not require any arguments. If it did, the necessary arguments would be passed as an array.

The unit test is a bit complex, and I have shown you the simplest example ever! Based on this example and my warning, you should be able to weigh the pros and cons of testing private methods. Last, you can also turn your private classes/methods into internal classes, which I will discuss in the next section!

Dealing with Internal Classes and Methods

Internal classes and methods help **encapsulate implementation details**, keeping them hidden from external consumers while maintaining a clean and controlled public API. They prevent **accidental usage of unstable code**, reduce **breaking changes**, and allow **refactoring flexibility** without affecting dependent projects. Internal components also enable unit testing via the *InternalsVisibleTo* attribute, ensuring testability without exposing unnecessary details. The *InternalsVisibleTo* attribute should be at the beginning of the source code, in the file that contains the internal classes/ methods to make them visible to the test project.

Instead of applying *InternalsVisibleTo* directly in the code, you can configure it in the **project file** (*.csproj*). This approach is cleaner and avoids modifying source files. Listing 4-23 shows the internal *StringHelpers* class and its *Capitalize* internal method. To make it visible to the *Apress. UnitTests* project, I have added the attribute at the beginning of the file after *using* statements.

Listing 4-23. The StringHelpers class

```
using System.Globalization;
using System.Runtime.CompilerServices;

[assembly: InternalsVisibleTo("Apress.UnitTests"), Internals
VisibleTo("AnotherAssembly1")]
[assembly: InternalsVisibleTo("AnotherAssembly2")]
namespace Apress.UnitTests.Internal;

internal static class StringHelpers
{
    internal static string Capitalize(string input)
    {
        if (string.IsNullOrEmpty(input)) return input;
        return CultureInfo.CurrentCulture.TextInfo.ToTitleCase
        (input.ToLower());
    }
}
```

You can apply the *InternalsVisibleTo* attribute multiple times. As demonstrated above, it can be written on a single line with entries separated by commas or placed on separate lines.

You can do the same to your project file as shown in the following:

```
<ItemGroup>
    <InternalsVisibleTo Include="Apress.UnitTests" />
    <InternalsVisibleTo Include="AnotherAssembly1" />
    <InternalsVisibleTo Include="AnotherAssembly2" />
</ItemGroup>
```

After doing that, you should be able to unit test any internal class and its internal methods. Listing 4-24 proves it by showing the *StringHelpersTests* class.

Listing 4-24. The StringHelpersTests class

```
using Apress.UnitTests.Internal;
using FluentAssertions;
using Xunit;

namespace Apress.UnitTests.InternalClasses;

public class StringHelpersTests
{
    [Fact]
    public void Capitalize_WhenAnInputIsProvidedtoCapitalize
    Method_ShouldCapitalizeCorrectlyInput()
    {
        // Arrange
        var input = "anthony";

        // Act
        var result = StringHelpers.Capitalize(input);
```

```
    // Assert
    result.Should().Be("Anthony");
  }
}
```

You can believe me, it's compiling, and the test passes!

Caution   Making an internal class visible to another assembly, as shown above, does not eliminate the need to reference the project in which the class is defined. You must still add the project containing the internal class as a reference in the target project.

Dealing with Abstract Classes and Virtual Methods

As you may know, abstract classes are classes that cannot be instantiated on their own and are designed to be inherited from. They often contain abstract methods—methods without an implementation—which compel derived classes to provide their own specific implementations, ensuring a consistent interface. Virtual methods, however, come with a default implementation in the base class but can be overridden in subclasses to customize behavior. Abstract classes and virtual methods promote code reuse, flexibility, and polymorphism in object-oriented programming, making it easier to maintain and extend software systems.

Unit testing abstract classes and virtual methods are challenging because they can't be instantiated directly and require concrete implementations or mocks to simulate their behavior, and I will show you how. Listing 4-25 shows the *Employee* abstract class, which stores the *name* and *employee* properties. It also defines the *CalculateSalary* abstract method and the virtual *DisplayInfo* method.

Listing 4-25. The Employee class

```
namespace Apress.UnitTests.AbstractClasses;

public abstract class Employee
{
    private string _name;
    private int _employee;

    public Employee(string name, int employeeId)
    {
        _name = name;
        _employee = employeeId;
    }

    public abstract decimal CalculateSalary();

    public virtual string DisplayInfo()
    {
        return $"Employee ID: {_name}, Name: {_employee}";
    }
}
```

There are two main approaches to unit test an abstract class:

1. **Test-Specific Derived Class**:

   Create a concrete subclass that implements the abstract methods. This lets you instantiate the class and test the behavior of its concrete methods directly.

2. **Mocking Framework**:

   Use a framework like NSubstitute to automatically create a derived class mock. Then, you will have access to the virtual class.

Your question is, "What method to choose?" Well, I suggest you do both. If you have a derived class, you should unit test it, obviously. If your abstract class contains virtual methods, you can unit test the abstract class and its virtual methods with a mocking framework. Let's use NSubstitute again to test a virtual method with its base implementation. Listing 4-26 shows the *EmployeeTests* class that unit test, via NSubstitute, the *Employee* class and its virtual *DisplayInfo* method.

Listing 4-26. The EmployeeTests class

```
using AutoFixture;
using FluentAssertions;
using NSubstitute;
using Xunit;

namespace Apress.UnitTests.AbstractClasses;

public class EmployeeTests
{
    [Fact]
    public void DisplayInfo_WhenDisplayInfoIsInvoked_
    ShouldDisplayInfoCorrectly()
    {
        var fixture = new Fixture();
        var name = fixture.Create<string>();
        var id = fixture.Create<int>();
        var employeeSubstitute = Substitute.ForPartsOf
        <Employee>(name, id);

        // Act
        string info = employeeSubstitute.DisplayInfo();
```

```
    // Assert
    info.Should().Be($"Employee Name: {name}, Id: {id}");
  }
}
```

Instead of using the *Substitute.For* method here, I used the *Substitute.ForPartsOf* method (which takes the employee's name and id as parameters and passes them to the constructor) to create a class that mocks the abstract *Employee* class. In reality, NSubstitute can create a derived class that serves as a mock and allows access to the virtual *DisplayInfo* method. It's magical, isn't it? As you can see, NSubstitute is really handy! So if you want to test your derived classes as well as the virtual methods (with their base implementation), I suggest combining the two approaches I showed you! You won't tear your hair out trying to figure out how to do it!

Dealing with HttpClients

There are different types of data access. For example, HTTP data access (such as REST APIs) can be performed using *HttpClient*, the go-to .NET class for sending HTTP requests, enabling modern applications to easily interact with external REST APIs. Its high-level, asynchronous API simplifies network communication.

There are two ways to implement *HttpClient*: either by injecting the *HttpClient* class through a typed client or by using a named client via the *IHttpClientFactory* interface injected as a dependency. This interface also allows you to create clients on the fly without invoking a predefined *HttpClient* in your configuration. I won't re-explain how these approaches work, as the focus is on unit testing. For more details on these approaches, I recommend reading this excellent post: https://medium.com/@marijatopalova123/understanding-httpclient-in-asp-net-basics-named-typed-and-refit-generated-clients-4e10ea967eed.

The *HttpClient* depends on the *HttpMessageHandler* object, which controls how HTTP requests are handled. In practice, we won't mock the HttpClient; we will mock instead the *HttpMessageHandler*. We can do that by using NSubstitute or simplify this step by using the RichardSzalay. MockHttp library. The RichardSzalay.MockHttp library simplifies testing by abstracting away the complexities of *HttpMessageHandler*, allowing you to focus on the logic of your code rather than the intricacies of HTTP communication. I recommend this, and I will use that library for my examples. To download it, run the following command:

```
NuGet\Install-Package RichardSzalay.MockHttp
```

Testing HttpClient

Consider the *BlogService* class, which implements the *GetPostsAsync* method to retrieve a list of blog posts. This service returns a list of strings containing the URLs of any blog posts it fetches; if no posts are fetched, it returns an empty list. For simplicity, JSON serialization hasn't been abstracted in this example. However, abstracting JSON serialization is generally a best practice since it allows you to change the serializer easily and mock its behavior in the calling class. Listing 4-27 displays the *BlogService* class.

Listing 4-27. The BlogService class

```
using System.Text.Json;

namespace Apress.UnitTests.HttpClients;

public class BlogService
{
    private readonly HttpClient _httpClient;

    public BlogService(HttpClient httpClient)
```

```
    {
        _httpClient = httpClient;
    }

    public async Task<List<string>> GetPostsAsync()
    {
        var response = await _httpClient.GetAsync("https://
        anthonygiretti/api/articles");
        var json = await response.Content.ReadAsStringAsync();

        if (json is null)
            return new List<string>();
        return JsonSerializer.Deserialize<List<string>>(json);
    }
}
```

Next, let's write the associated unit test. Listing 4-28 shows the *BlogServiceTests* class with its test method *GetPostsAsync_WhenGetPostsAsyncReturnsBlogPostsAsString_ShouldReturnAListOfStrings*.

Listing 4-28. The BlogServiceTests class

```
using AutoFixture;
using ExpectedObjects;
using RichardSzalay.MockHttp;
using System.Text.Json;
using Xunit;

namespace Apress.UnitTests.HttpClients;

public class BlogServiceTests
{
    [Fact]
    public async Task GetPostsAsync_WhenGetPostsAsyncReturns
    BlogPostsAsString_ShouldReturnAListOfStrings()
```

```
    {
        // Arrange
        var fixture = new Fixture();
        var urls = fixture.CreateMany<string>(2);
        var stringfiedUrls = JsonSerializer.Serialize(urls);

        var mockHttp = new MockHttpMessageHandler();
        mockHttp.When("https://anthonygiretti/api/articles")
                .Respond("application/json", stringfiedUrls);
        var client = new HttpClient(mockHttp);
        var blogService = new BlogService(client);
        var expectedResult = urls.ToList().ToExpectedObject();

        // Act
        var result  = await blogService.GetPostsAsync();

        // Assert
        expectedResult.ShouldEqual(result);
    }
}
```

Since we are using a fake *HttpMessageHandler* (*MockHttpMessage Handler*) from the RichardSzalay.MockHttp library, we are limited in the parameters we can use.

First, the **URL of the endpoint** being called must be the same as the one passed in the *HttpClient* class, meaning the URL "https://anthonygiretti/api/articles", which we provide to the *When* method of the RichardSzalay.MockHttp library.

Next, the **Content-Type** must be **application/json** (passed to the *Respond* function of RichardSzalay.MockHttp) so that *HttpClient* consumes the data in JSON format. This is not something that can be mocked arbitrarily.

To **simulate the results returned by** *HttpClient*, we can generate any string using AutoFixture and then serialize it with **System.Text.Json** to mimic an HTTP response (via the *Respond* method of RichardSzalay. MockHttp).

Then, I instantiate the *SUT (System Under Test)*, which is the *BlogService* class, and define the expected list of strings using ExpectedObjects.

That's it! You see, it's simple!

Testing HttpClient via IHttpClientFactory

The use of *IHttpClientFactory* is very simple. There is only one small difference compared with using *HttpClient* directly. When *IHttpClientFactory* is injected into a class constructor, you just need to use the *CreateClient* method to obtain an *HttpClient*. After that, everything remains the same, as shown earlier. Listing 4-29 shows the *TagsService* class, which takes *IHttpClientFactory* in its constructor. The functionality of this class is similar to what we previously saw with the *BlogService* class.

Listing 4-29. The TagsService class

```
using System.Text.Json;

namespace Apress.UnitTests.HttpClients;

public class TagsService
{
    private readonly IHttpClientFactory _httpClientFactory;

    public TagsService(IHttpClientFactory httpClientFactory)
    {
        _httpClientFactory = httpClientFactory;
    }
```

```
public async Task<List<string>> GetTagsAsync()
{
    var httpClient = _httpClientFactory.CreateClient();
    var response = await httpClient.GetAsync("https://
    anthonygiretti/api/tags");
    var json = await response.Content.ReadAsStringAsync();

    if (json == null)
        return new List<string>();
    return JsonSerializer.Deserialize<List<string>>(json);
}
}
```

The unit test is also very similar to the *BlogServiceTests* class seen previously. The only difference lies in the fact that we need to mock the *IHttpClientFactory*, simulating the *CreateClient* method to return an *HttpClient* that takes the *MockHttpMessageHandler* class as a parameter. Listing 4-30 shows the *TagsServiceTests* class and its test method named *GetTagsAsync_WhenGetTagsAsyncReturnsTagsAsString_ShouldReturnAListOfStrings*.

Listing 4-30. The TagsServiceTests class

```
using AutoFixture;
using ExpectedObjects;
using NSubstitute;
using RichardSzalay.MockHttp;
using System.Text.Json;
using Xunit;

namespace Apress.UnitTests.HttpClients;
```

```csharp
public class TagsServiceTests
{
    [Fact]
    public async Task GetTagsAsync_WhenGetTagsAsyncReturns
    TagsAsString_ShouldReturnAListOfStrings()
    {
        // Arrange
        var fixture = new Fixture();
        var tags = fixture.CreateMany<string>(5);
        var stringfiedTags = JsonSerializer.Serialize(tags);

        var mockHttp = new MockHttpMessageHandler();
        mockHttp.When("https://anthonygiretti/api/tags")
                .Respond("application/json", stringfiedTags);

        var httpClientFactory = Substitute.For<IHttpClient
        Factory>();
        var client = new HttpClient(mockHttp);
        httpClientFactory.CreateClient().Returns(client);

        var tagsService = new TagsService(httpClientFactory);
        var expectedResult = tags.ToList().ToExpectedObject();

        // Act
        var result = await tagsService.GetTagsAsync();

        // Assert
        expectedResult.ShouldEqual(result);
    }
}
```

It's simple, isn't it? 😊

Dealing with Infrastructure Components

So far, I haven't shown you any unit test about infrastructure components and frameworks (except *HttpClients*) like ASP.NET Core Web API controllers, ASP.NET Core middleware, and data access layers (SQL, Entity Framework, etc.) because it is generally not worth it for several reasons:

1. These components are integration points, not pure logic.

    -   Unit tests are designed to test isolated units of logic. However, infrastructure components rely on external dependencies like databases, HTTP requests, or the framework itself.

    -   **Controllers**: Mostly act as a bridge between HTTP and the business logic. They contain minimal logic beyond routing and request handling.

    -   **Middleware**: Often handle cross-cutting concerns (e.g., logging, authentication) and rely heavily on the framework.

    -   **Data Access Layers**: Interact with databases, and testing them in isolation requires heavy mocking, which often leads to brittle tests.

2. Excessive mocking makes tests brittle and unrealistic.

    -   To unit test these components, you often need to mock everything (e.g., DbContext, HTTP context, dependency injection).

- Mocking Entity Framework (DbContext) or SQL operations leads to tests that don't reflect real-world database behavior (e.g., transactions, constraints, query performance).

- Over-mocking results in false positives—tests pass, but the real application may still fail due to incorrect assumptions.

In summary, testing framework behavior is unnecessary. When working with databases like Entity Framework Core, using an in-memory database is a more suitable approach than unit or even integration testing. For ASP.NET Core Web APIs, controllers and middleware should be validated through end-to-end tests. As for the rest of the application, the focus should be on unit testing the business logic. This means that you won't achieve 100% unit test coverage across your application, which is perfectly fine.

Summary

In this chapter, you have explored unit testing in .NET by addressing challenges such as mocking *DataTable*, managing *DateTime*, testing *HttpClient*, and working with abstract and private methods. You also discovered specialized libraries for specific scenarios, such as FakeLogger for testing *ILogger* and RichardSzalay.MockHttp for *HttpClient*. With a solid understanding of AutoFixture, FluentAssertions, ExpectedObjects, NSubstitute, and these additional tools, you should now be well-equipped to tackle any unit testing scenario.

CHAPTER 5

Automating Unit Tests

Automating unit tests ensures faster feedback, consistency, scalability, and early bug detection while boosting developer productivity and supporting CI/CD pipelines. Measuring code coverage helps identify untested areas, reduces risks, and improves confidence in code changes. It optimizes testing efforts and ensures critical functionality is verified, enhancing software reliability. While 100% coverage isn't always necessary, maintaining meaningful test coverage leads to more maintainable and high-quality code. In this chapter, I will show you how to

- Automate your unit tests in Visual Studio.

- Automate unit tests with Azure DevOps.

- Measure the code coverage.

Automate Your Unit Tests in Visual Studio

Visual Studio provides a powerful feature for automating unit tests: **Live Unit Testing**. This real-time feature automatically runs unit tests in the background as you modify your code, offering instant feedback by highlighting covered and uncovered sections while displaying test results inline. It streamlines development by catching bugs early, minimizing manual test execution, and ensuring code changes are continuously validated. By maintaining ongoing test coverage without manual effort, Live Unit Testing enhances both development speed and confidence.

© Anthony Giretti 2025
A. Giretti, *The Unit Testing Practice Cookbook*,
https://doi.org/10.1007/979-8-8688-1454-9_5

Caution   Live Unit Testing is available in **Visual Studio Enterprise edition**, starting from **Visual Studio 2017 and later versions** (including 2019 and 2022). It is **not available** in the Community or Professional edition.

To get started, a few clicks will be necessary, but rest assured, the process is quite simple, even though it involves navigating through a few screens. As mentioned in Chapter 3, unit tests can be executed in the Test Explorer window. So return to Test Explorer and click the Live Unit Testing Window icon, as shown in Figure 5-1.

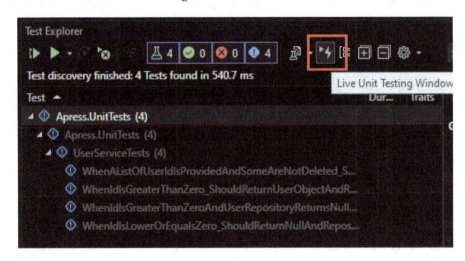

Figure 5-1. *Opening Live Unit Testing Window*

After clicking, the following window in Figure 5-2 will appear, where you need to complete two steps: First, click the "Include all tests" link to enable Live Unit Testing for all existing unit tests. Once this is done, click the green arrow, as illustrated in Figure 5-2.

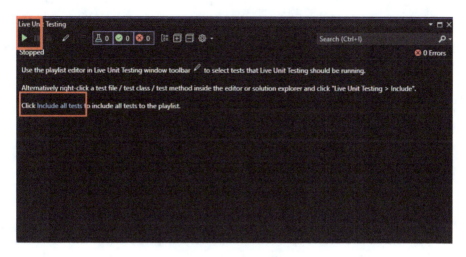

Figure 5-2. *Activating Live Unit Testing*

Next, you will be prompted to configure Live Unit Testing as shown in Figure 5-3.

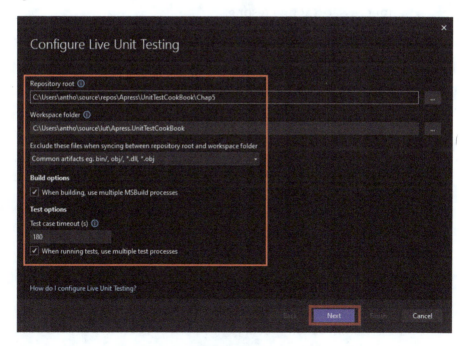

Figure 5-3. *Configuring Live Unit Testing*

The Live Unit Testing configuration window shown in Figure 5-3 allows you to set up Live Unit Testing in Visual Studio by specifying key settings. Here's what each option means:

- **Repository Root**: This defines the root directory of your project repository. It ensures that Live Unit Testing has access to the correct source code location.

- **Workspace Folder**: This specifies the directory where Live Unit Testing will store its temporary files and test results.

- **Exclude Files**: This option allows you to specify files that should be ignored during synchronization between the repository root and the workspace folder. The dropdown includes common artifacts such as bin/, .obj/, *.dll, and *.obj, which are typically unnecessary for unit testing.

- **Build Options—Use Multiple MSBuild Processes**: Enabling this option allows Visual Studio to use multiple MSBuild processes while building the project, which can improve performance for larger projects.

- **Test Options**:

  - **Test Case Timeout (s)**: Specifies the maximum time (in seconds) that a test case can run before it is considered a failure due to timeout. The default is set to **180 seconds**.

  - **Use Multiple Test Processes**: When enabled, this allows Visual Studio to run multiple tests simultaneously in different processes, enhancing test execution speed.

Typically, no modifications are needed here. Personally, I've never had to change anything in this setup. Therefore, I recommend clicking the **Next** button immediately to proceed.

The next window will present Step 2 of the Live Unit Testing configuration, as illustrated in Figure 5-4.

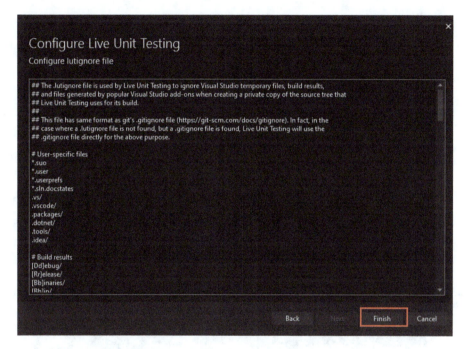

Figure 5-4. *Configuring Live Unit Testing (Step 2)*

This step in the Live Unit Testing configuration allows you to configure the *.lutignore* file, which defines files and directories that should be excluded from Live Unit Testing operations. Here's what it does:

1. **Ignores Temporary and Unnecessary Files**: The **.lutignore** file is used to exclude temporary Visual Studio files, build outputs, and other artifacts generated during the development process. This prevents Live Unit Testing from scanning irrelevant files, improving performance.

2. **Uses Git Ignore Syntax**: The **.lutignore** file follows the same syntax as a **.gitignore** file, making it easy to manage exclusions. If a **.lutignore** file is not present, Live Unit Testing will automatically use the **.gitignore** file instead.

3. **Optimizes Live Unit Testing Performance**: By ignoring unnecessary files such as bin/, obj/, .vs/, .dotnet/, and *.userprefs, the testing process runs more efficiently without analyzing files that don't contribute to test execution.

Once again, there's nothing you need to modify here—at least, I've never had to make any changes. Simply click the Finish button to complete the Live Unit Testing setup and activate it for your project.

Live Unit Testing is now enabled. As you write new unit tests or modify existing ones, they will automatically run as long as your code compiles. Figure 5-5 illustrates the editing of the *DeleteByIdsAsync* method within the *UserService* class, where a new instruction has been added, triggering the execution of the already written unit tests.

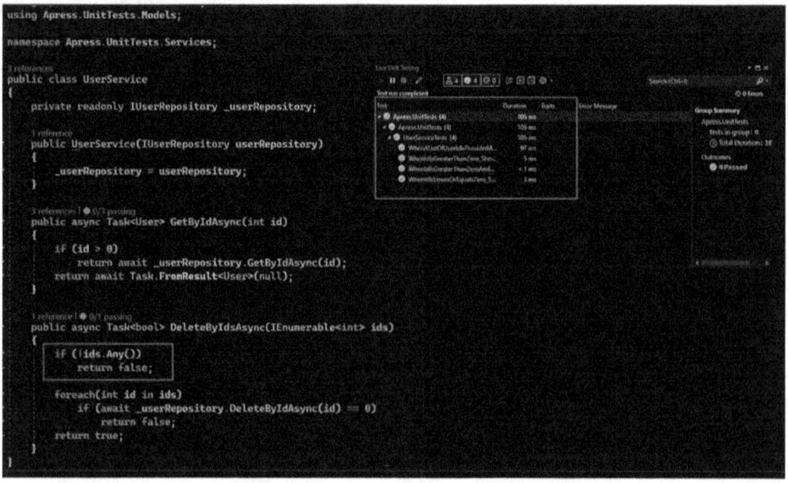

Figure 5-5. *Live Unit Testing in action*

You can now track all changes to your code in real time and see their impact on your unit tests!

Automate Your Unit Tests in Azure DevOps
What's Azure DevOps?

Azure DevOps is a cloud-based DevOps platform by Microsoft that provides a comprehensive set of tools for software development, collaboration, and deployment. It enables organizations to plan, develop, test, and deliver applications more efficiently using modern DevOps practices. Azure DevOps provides the following features:

1. **Azure Repos**: Provides version control tools for tracking code changes, supporting both Git repositories and Team Foundation Version Control (TFVC) while enabling collaboration through pull requests, branching strategies, and code reviews.

2. **Azure Pipelines**: It's a *CI/CD (continuous integration and continuous deployment)* tool that automates builds and deployments, supporting multiple languages and platforms such as .NET, Java, Python, Node.js, and Docker.

3. **Azure Boards**: Provides a powerful project management and agile development tool that supports Kanban boards, Scrum boards, dashboards, and backlog tracking while offering custom reporting and analytics to monitor project progress effectively.

4. **Azure Test Plans**: Provides a comprehensive testing tool for managing test cases and executing both manual and automated tests, offering end-to-end traceability from requirements to test execution results while supporting load testing and exploratory testing.

5. **Azure Artifacts**: Provides a package management system that enables secure storage and sharing of NuGet, npm, Maven, and Python packages, allowing teams to reuse dependencies across projects while integrating seamlessly with Azure Pipelines for efficient artifact management.

In this chapter, I will focus solely on Azure Repos and Azure Pipelines, demonstrating how to build a YAML pipeline for continuous integration without including application deployment examples. The goal is to concentrate entirely on unit test automation.

A YAML pipeline in Azure DevOps is a code-based, declarative approach to defining CI/CD workflows using a YAML file. Unlike the traditional graphical editor, YAML pipelines enable developers to define build, test, and deployment processes as version-controlled code within a repository. These .yml files enhance reproducibility, portability, and maintainability, ensuring a consistent development workflow across different environments.

Getting Started with Azure DevOps

To get started with Azure DevOps, you will have to follow these steps:

1. Sign up on the address `https://azure.microsoft.com/en-us/products/devops/`.

2. Create an Organization and a Project.

3. Set up Repositories, Pipelines, Boards, and Test Plans.

4. Integrate with your existing DevOps workflow.

5. Automate your CI/CD pipeline and deploy applications.

I'll only showcase the CI (continuous integration) step in this chapter. If you want to learn more about it, how to set up a Git repository, which is mandatory to create a CI pipeline, you can go the following Microsoft documentation here: `https://learn.microsoft.com/en-us/azure/devops/get-started/?view=azure-devops`. This documentation will provide you all you need to get started, including how to set up a repository.

Creating a Continuous Integration Pipeline in Azure DevOps

Creating a CI pipeline requires several steps, such as creating the YAML file, uploading it along with the application's source code to Git, and then verifying the pipeline's functionality by executing it. Let's start by creating the YAML file.

Note   I'll only show how to build the .NET application and run the unit tests. I'd like to focus only on the unit tests even though the Azure DevOps pipeline allows many other tasks during a pipeline.

Creating the YAML File for the CI

Let's take a small ASP.NET Core application with some code, including a class that needs to be unit tested. The specific implementation of the application is not important here. Ensure that you have already created a unit test project that references this application. Now, proceed by creating a YAML file, for example, azure-pipeline.yml, which must be created at the root of your application, as illustrated in Figure 5-6.

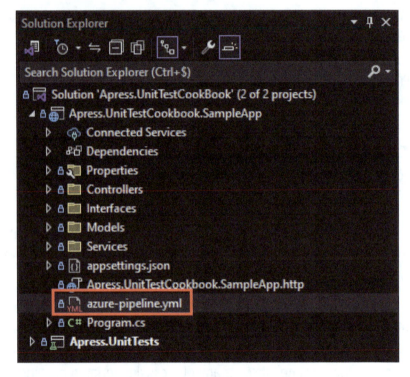

Figure 5-6. *The azure-pipeline.yml file*

Once created, let's define the instructions to compile the application and execute the unit tests. I'll focus only on the unit tests here and what's necessary to run them.

Listing 5-1 shows the *azure-pipeline.yml* file content. I'll explain its content after showing it to you.

Listing 5-1. The azure-pipeline.yml file

```
trigger:
  branches:
    include:
      - main
      - develop

pool:
  vmImage: 'windows-latest'

steps:
- checkout: self

- task: UseDotNet@2
  inputs:
    packageType: 'sdk'
    version: '9.x'

- task: DotNetCoreCLI@2
  displayName: 'Build Function App'
  inputs:
    command: 'build'
    projects: '**/Apress.UnitTestCookbook.SampleApp.csproj'
    arguments: '--configuration Release'

- task: DotNetCoreCLI@2
  displayName: 'Run unit tests'
  inputs:
   command: test
   projects: '**/Apress.UnitTests.csproj'
   arguments: '--configuration $(buildConfiguration)'
```

Explanations:

This Azure DevOps YAML pipeline automates the build and testing of an application whenever changes are pushed to specific branches. The list below explains all the steps by order:

1. **Trigger** (*trigger*): The pipeline runs automatically when code is pushed to the main or develop branches.

2. **Build Agent** (*pool*): Uses a Windows-based virtual machine to execute the pipeline.

3. **Repository Checkout** (*checkout*): Fetches the latest version of the repository into the pipeline workspace.

4. **Install .NET SDK** (*UseDotNet@2*): Installs the required .NET SDK (version 9.x) for building and testing.

5. **Build Application** (*DotNetCoreCLI@2 - build*): Compiles the application in Release mode, targeting the specified project.

6. **Run Unit Tests** (*DotNetCoreCLI@2 - test*): Executes unit tests using dotnet test on the designated test project.

These commands provide a simple way to run a build pipeline, including unit test execution. I don't want you to feel overwhelmed, but if you aspire to become an expert in YAML schema references, you can explore them in this Microsoft documentation page: `https://learn.microsoft.com/en-us/azure/devops/pipelines/yaml-schema/?view=azure-pipelines`.

Uploading Your Project to Your Git Repository

Now, it's time to create a Git repository and upload it to Azure Repos.Since this book is not focused on Git itself, I'll show the simplest way to create a repository from Visual Studio. To do so, click the "Add to Source Control" button and then the "Git" button at the bottom right of Visual Studio as shown in Figure 5-7.

Figure 5-7. *The "Add to Source Control" button and the "Git" button*

You will be prompted to set up the project from which you want to create a repository. In the left panel, select "Azure DevOps" and then log into your Azure DevOps account. The repository name and project will be automatically generated based on your Visual Studio solution name, as shown in Figure 5-8.

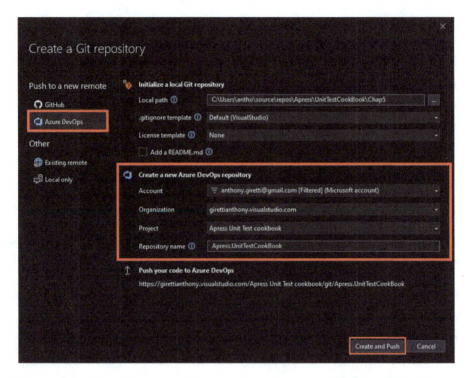

Figure 5-8. *The "Create a Git repository" prompt in Visual Studio*

Next, click the "Create and Push" button. This will create
your repository in Azure DevOps and push your application to it
simultaneously. Now, navigate to Azure DevOps, and locate the "Pipelines"
link. Since no pipeline exists yet, you'll need to create one by clicking the
"Create Pipeline" button, as shown in Figure 5-9.

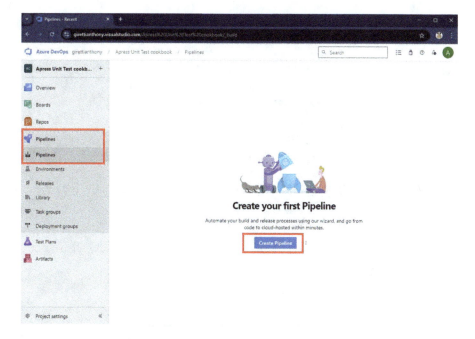

Figure 5-9. *The "Create Pipeline" button in Azure DevOps*

Azure DevOps will prompt you to specify the location of your code. Since it is stored in Azure DevOps, simply click the "Azure Repos Git (YAML)" button, as shown in Figure 5-10.

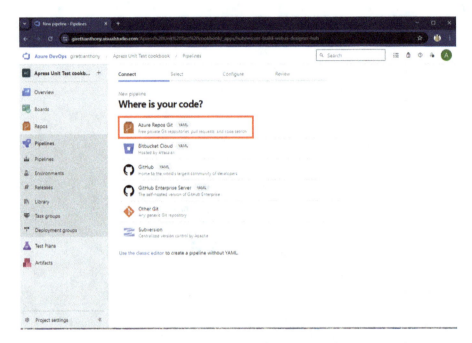

Figure 5-10. *Selecting Azure Repos Git as code source*

Next, a list of all your repositories will be displayed. Select the desired repository, as illustrated in Figure 5-11.

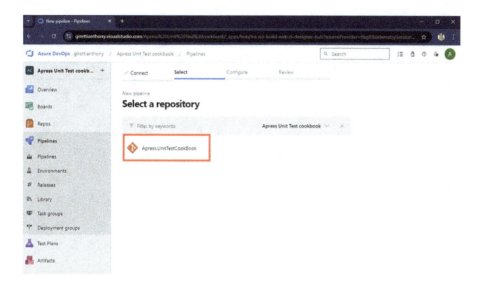

Figure 5-11. *Selecting the desired repository*

You will then be prompted to configure your pipeline. Since the YAML file has already been created, select "Existing Azure Pipelines YAML file," as it is already written and configured for your .NET project. This step is illustrated in Figure 5-12.

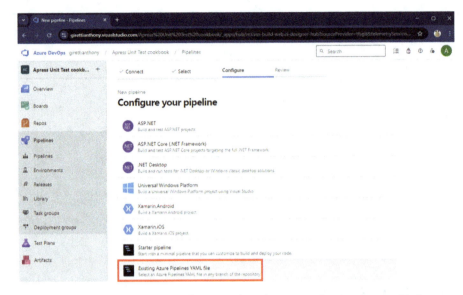

Figure 5-12. *Selecting the "Existing Azure Pipelines YAML file"*
configuration

Azure DevOps will prompt you to specify the location of your YAML
file. Simply select it from the dropdown menu, as shown in Figure 5-13.

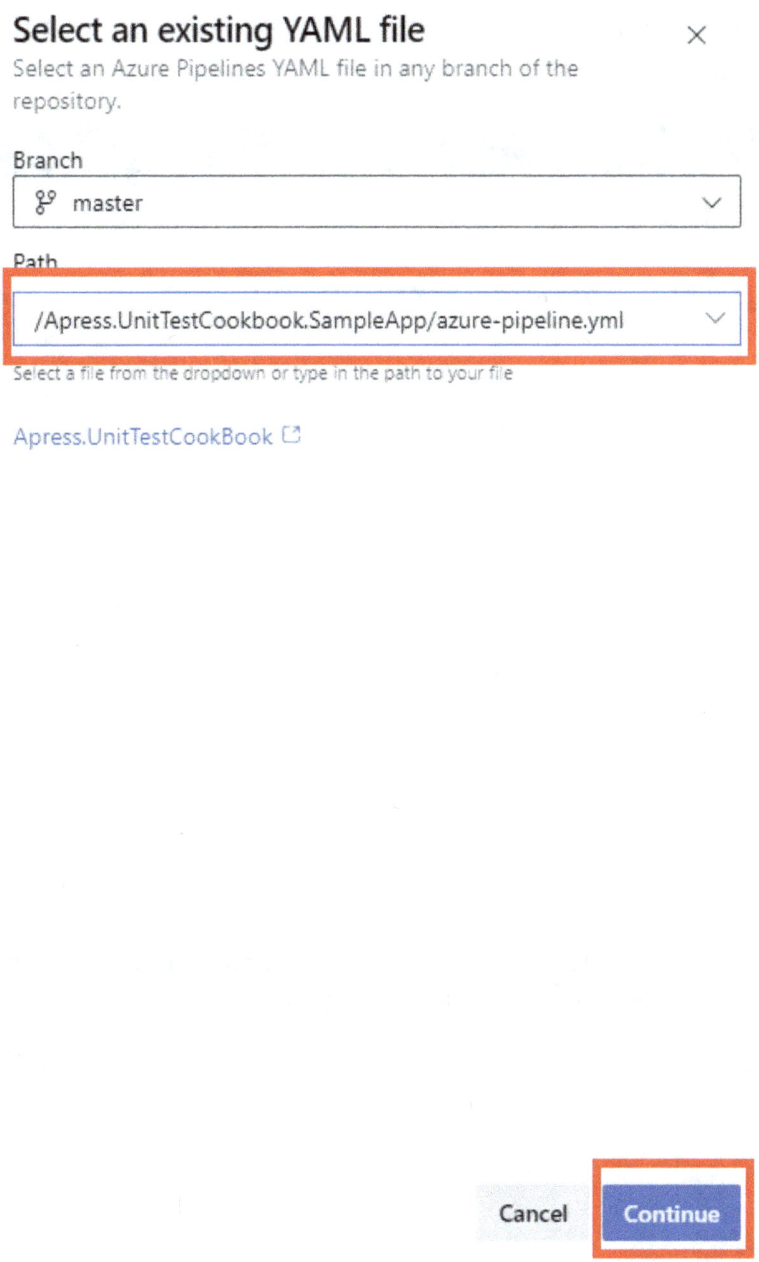

Select an existing YAML file   ✕

Select an Azure Pipelines YAML file in any branch of the
repository.

Branch

⎇ master   ⌄

Path

/Apress.UnitTestCookbook.SampleApp/azure-pipeline.yml   ⌄

Select a file from the dropdown or type in the path to your file

Apress.UnitTestCookBook ⌕

Cancel   **Continue**

Figure 5-13. *Retrieving the YAML file*

Next, click the "Continue" button, and Azure DevOps will display your YAML file. If needed, you can edit it; otherwise, simply click the "Run" button, as shown in Figure 5-14.

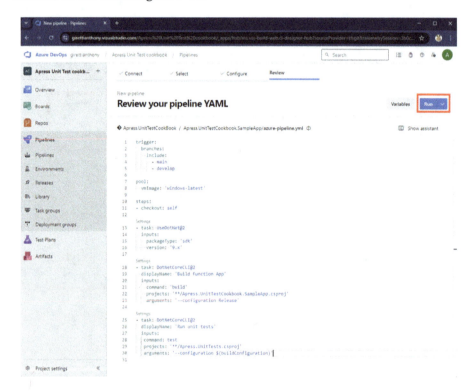

Figure 5-14. *Reviewing the YAML file and running the pipeline*

You will be redirected to the build page, where you can monitor the build details, as demonstrated in Figure 5-15.

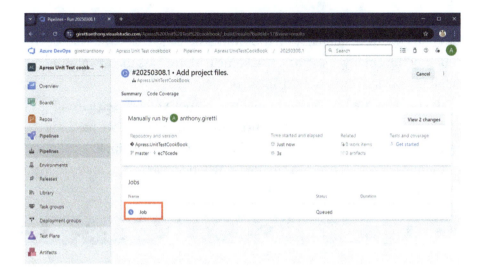

Figure 5-15. *The build details page*

Verifying the Pipeline Execution Results

If you have previously clicked the "Job" button, you'll be able to track the task results as shown in Figure 5-16.

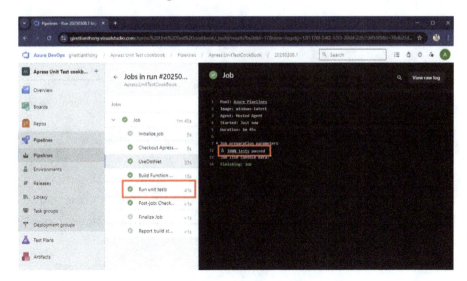

Figure 5-16. *The task execution result*

From there you can check any task (that you defined in your YAML file) and its logs. Specifically on the "Run unit tests" tasks, you can see the details of how many tests passed; if some had not passed, the number of failed tests would have been displayed.

If you navigate back to the "Pipelines" panel, you will see a list of all pipelines that have run or are currently running. Since we have set up a trigger on the "main" and "develop" branches, the pipeline will automatically run and appear in the list whenever a push is made to these branches, as shown in Figure 5-17.

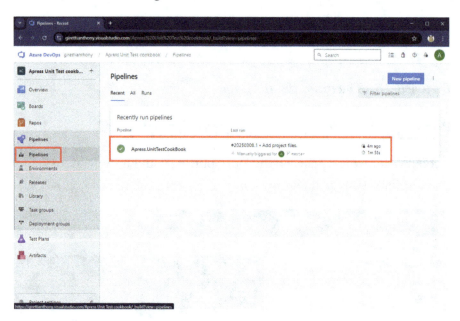

Figure 5-17. *Overview of completed and ongoing pipelines*

This represents a continuous integration pipeline, ensuring that every code change is automatically built, tested, and more if you decide to add features (e.g., creating an artifact) on it whenever a push is made to the monitored branches. 😊

Measure the Code Coverage

Implementing code coverage in a project, whether in Visual Studio or Azure DevOps, is crucial for ensuring code quality and reliability. It helps identify uncovered parts of the codebase, ensuring that critical logic is tested and reducing the risk of undetected bugs. In Visual Studio, developers can analyze coverage locally, improving their tests before committing changes. In Azure DevOps, integrating code coverage into CI pipelines provides continuous insights into test effectiveness, helping teams maintain high-quality code standards and catch regressions early. Code coverage implies two types of coverage: line coverage and branch coverage. I'll get back to this further in the section.

Measure the Code Coverage in Visual Studio

Measuring code coverage in Visual Studio is a simple process. The first step is to create an XML file with a *.runsettings* extension, which defines the code coverage settings. This file should be placed inside the unit test project. Let's name it *coverage.runsettings*.

The file structure would look like Listing 5-2.

Listing 5-2. The coverage.runsettings file template

```
<?xml version="1.0" encoding="utf-8"?>
<RunSettings>
    <DataCollectionRunSettings>
        <DataCollectors>
            <DataCollector friendlyName="Code Coverage">
                <Configuration>
                    <CodeCoverage>
                    </CodeCoverage>
```

```
            </Configuration>
          </DataCollector>
        </DataCollectors>
      </DataCollectionRunSettings>
</RunSettings>
```

The file is for now empty, but we will fill it out soon.

To further use in an Azure DevOps pipeline, let's configure its properties to set the Copy to Output Directory property to "Copy always." This file is not used by default by Visual Studio, so we need to let it know that this file should be considered for any unit test that needs to be configured with specific rules. To do so, go on the Test panel, then click the Configure Run Settings menu, and select "Auto Detect runsettings Files" as shown in Figure 5-18.

Figure 5-18. *Auto Detect runsettings Files*

The *coverage.runsettings* file is now known by Visual Studio.

Let's go now into the Test Explorer panel. Right-click the first unit test item at the top of the list and click the "Analyze Code Coverage" menu as shown in Figure 5-19.

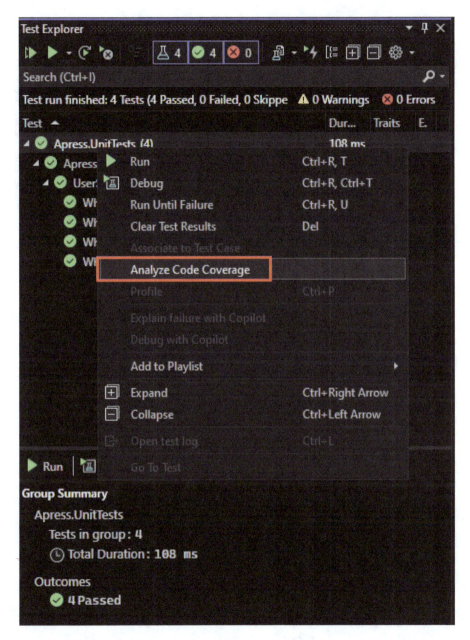

Figure 5-19. *Analyze Code Coverage*

This will trigger the unit test execution, and once done, Visual Studio will display the code coverage results at the bottom of the screen as shown in Figure 5-20.

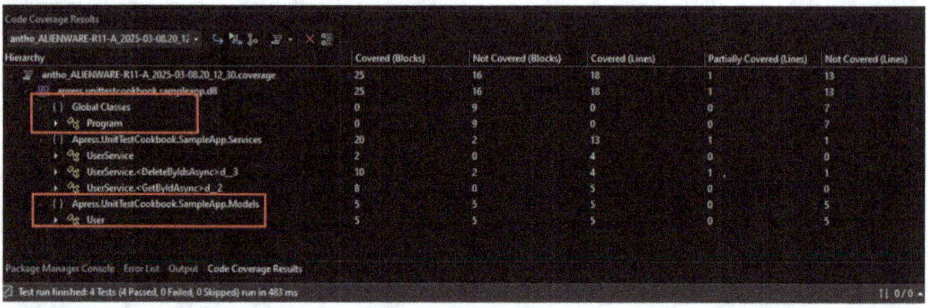

Figure 5-20. *The code coverage results*

Since I'm unit testing an ASP.NET Core application, all classes appear in the code coverage report—including files like *Program.cs* (which uses Top-Level Statements); models like the *User* class, which only contains properties; and the unit tests themselves. These files don't require unit testing, as there's nothing meaningful to test; also it's nonsense to include into the code coverage the tests themselves. To exclude them from the code coverage report, I can simply edit the *coverage.runsettings* file. Listing 5-3 shows the file edited as follows.

Listing 5-3. The updated coverage.runsettings file

```xml
<?xml version="1.0" encoding="utf-8"?>
<RunSettings>
    <DataCollectionRunSettings>
        <DataCollectors>
            <DataCollector friendlyName="Code Coverage">
                <Configuration>
                    <CodeCoverage>
                        <ModulePaths>
                            <Exclude>
```

```
            <ModulePath>apress.unittests.
            dll</ModulePath>
          </Exclude>
        </ModulePaths>
        <Functions>
          <Exclude>
            <Function>Program</Function>
          </Exclude>
        </Functions>
      </CodeCoverage>
    </Configuration>
   </DataCollector>
  </DataCollectors>
 </DataCollectionRunSettings>
</RunSettings>
```

The *ModulePaths* node excludes the entire *apress.unittests.dll* assembly from the coverage report; this means that any code *inside apress.unittests. dll* (which contains all the unit tests) will not be measured for test coverage. It could also be useful to exclude any other projects you don't want to measure coverage or even third-party libraries that don't need coverage.

The *Functions* node excludes the *Program.cs* file. The latter does not belong to any specific assembly; else, the syntax would have been something like this: *{namespace}.{filename}.cs*. You can add any exclusions as you want as long as you add a new node each time in the *Exclude* parent node. The reasoning is the same for both *ModulePaths* and *Functions* nodes. The last question you may have in mind is, "How do I exclude a class that has a namespace and a class name like the User class we want to exclude?" You can add it in the Functions name with the following syntax: *Apress.UnitTestCookbook.SampleApp.Models.User.cs*. However, it's not my favorite technique. I prefer to exclude it with an attribute named *ExcludeFromCodeCoverage* on the *User* class itself as shown in Listing 5-4.

Listing 5-4. The excluded User class

```
using System.Diagnostics.CodeAnalysis;

namespace Apress.UnitTestCookbook.SampleApp.Models;

[ExcludeFromCodeCoverage]
public class User
{
    public int Id { get; set; }
    public string FirstName { get; set; }
    public string LastName { get; set; }
    public string Email { get; set; }
    public bool IsActive { get; set; }
}
```

What happens if I measure the coverage again? We should see now the following as illustrated in Figure 5-21.

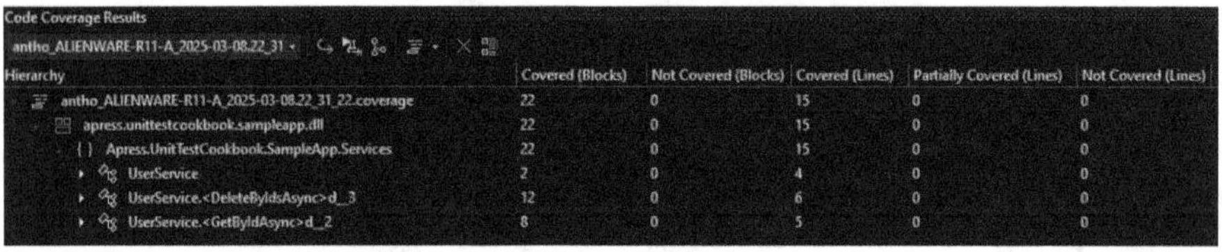

Figure 5-21. *The code coverage results without unwanted code*

The columns in the Code Coverage Results window in Visual Studio represent different aspects of how much of the code has been covered by unit tests. Here's what each column means:

1. **Covered** (Blocks)

   - The number of basic blocks (small units of execution) that were executed during tests.

   - A basic block is a straight-line sequence of instructions with no branches.

2. **Not Covered** (Blocks)

   - The number of basic blocks that were not executed by any test.

   - Indicates areas of the code that are completely untested.

3. **Covered** (Lines)

   - The number of lines of code that were executed at least once during the test run.

   - Helps in understanding the line-level coverage of the code.

4. **Partially Covered** (Lines)

   - The number of lines that were only partially covered.

   - This happens when a conditional statement (like if, else, or loops) executes only some of its possible paths.

5. **Not Covered** (Lines)

   - The number of lines of code that were never executed during the test run.

- Indicates the areas of the code that need additional test coverage.

Higher values for "Covered (Lines)" and "Covered (Blocks)" indicate better test coverage. If "Not Covered (Lines)" is high, additional unit tests should be written to improve coverage. Similarly, if "Partially Covered (Lines)" is high, ensure that tests cover all branches of conditional statements.

If we take as example the UserService class in its globality (which includes both methods), we might want to know the percentage of code coverage. Unfortunately, we must compute it ourselves. There are two ways to compute the percentage (from the blocks or from the lines) by using the followings formulas as shown in Figure 5-22.

$$\text{Code Coverage (\%)} = \left(\frac{\text{Covered Blocks}}{\text{Covered Blocks} + \text{Not Covered Blocks}} \right) \times 100$$

or equivalently:

$$\text{Code Coverage (\%)} = \left(\frac{\text{Covered Lines}}{\text{Covered Lines} + \text{Not Covered Lines}} \right) \times 100$$

Figure 5-22. *The code coverage formulas*

Code coverage results may vary slightly depending on whether you measure blocks or lines, with line-based coverage generally providing more accuracy. So how can you improve your coverage? Here's how:

1. Identify untested code using the "Not Covered (Lines)" column.

2. Write more unit tests to cover missing scenarios.

3. Ensure all branches of conditions (if/else, loops) are tested.

You can appreciate test coverage and improve it if needed. Additionally, if you want to view your coverage in Azure DevOps, the next section will guide you through the process.

Measure the Code Coverage in Azure DevOps

Publishing code coverage in Azure DevOps enhances visibility, ensures code quality, and helps identify untested areas. It automates coverage tracking, integrates with CI/CD workflows, and enables quality gates to prevent untested code from being deployed. Microsoft.NET.Test.Sdk provides a built-in capability to run with Azure DevOps, and setting in code coverage on the latter is pretty straightforward. What we need is to update the YAML file in your .NET application as shown in Listing 5-5.

Listing 5-5. The updated YAML file

```
trigger:
  branches:
    include:
        - main
        - master
        - develop

pool:
  vmImage: 'windows-latest'

steps:
- checkout: self

- task: UseDotNet@2
  inputs:
    packageType: 'sdk'
    version: '9.x'
```

```
- task: DotNetCoreCLI@2
  displayName: 'Build Sample App'
  inputs:
    command: 'build'
    projects: '**/Apress.UnitTestCookbook.SampleApp.csproj'
    arguments: '--configuration Release'
- task: DotNetCoreCLI@2
  displayName: 'Run unit tests'
  inputs:
    command: test
    projects: '**/Apress.UnitTests.csproj'
    arguments: '--configuration $(buildConfiguration) --settings
    $(Build.SourcesDirectory)/UnitTestCookBook/coverage.
    runsettings --collect "Code Coverage"'
```

I have put in bold instructions to tell Azure DevOps where to locate, with the --settings command, the *coverage.runsettings* file (which is needed if you want to customize your code coverage report) and also enable the code coverage report with the --collect command; the latter takes a parameter value "Code Coverage". That's it! If we go again in Azure Devops, find the build of the just-run pipeline, and click the Code Coverage panel, we'll see the code coverage percentage as shown in Figure 5-23.

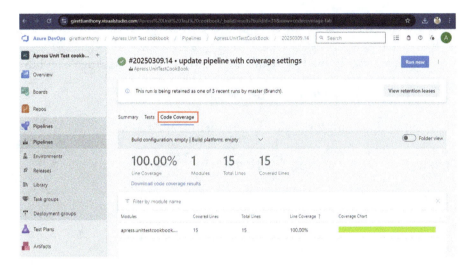

Figure 5-23. *The code coverage in Azure DevOps*

As you can see, the code coverage is divided by assembly, making it easy to identify areas where the application lacks sufficient test coverage.

Going Further with the Best Tools

I showed you the built-in code coverage report brought by the Microsoft. NET.Test.Sdk. However, there is an alternative named Coverlet. Coverlet is a code coverage tool for .NET, which provides the following capabilities:

1. Cross-platform and CI/CD-friendly

2. Supports multiple report formats

3. Easier integration with dotnet test

4. Better exclusion and filtering options

5. More flexible and actively maintained

For modern .NET projects, Coverlet is the best choice for code coverage in Azure DevOps and any other CI/CD pipeline platforms.

Let's see together how to enable it in your project and then deploy it into Azure DevOps.

First of all, you'll need to install the required NuGet package as follows:

```
NuGet\Install-Package coverlet.msbuild
```

Then update your YAML file as shown in Listing 5-6.

Listing 5-6. The updated YAML file with Coverlet

```yaml
trigger:
  branches:
    include:
      - main
      - master
      - develop

pool:
  vmImage: 'windows-latest'

steps:
- checkout: self

- task: UseDotNet@2
  inputs:
    packageType: 'sdk'
    version: '9.x'

- task: DotNetCoreCLI@2
  displayName: 'Build Sample App'
  inputs:
    command: 'build'
    projects: '**/Apress.UnitTestCookbook.SampleApp.csproj'
```

```
    arguments: '--configuration Release'

- task: DotNetCoreCLI@2
  displayName: 'dotnet test'
  inputs:
    command: 'test'
    arguments: '--configuration $(buildConfiguration)
/p:CollectCoverage=true /p:CoverletOutputFormat=cobertura'
    publishTestResults: true
    projects: '**/Apress.UnitTests.csproj'

- task: PublishCodeCoverageResults@2
  displayName: 'Publish code coverage report'
  inputs:
    codeCoverageTool: 'Cobertura'
    summaryFileLocation: '**/*coverage.cobertura.xml'
```

As you can see, I have updated the test section with the Coverlet configuration. The parameters /p:CollectCoverage=true and /p:Cover letOutputFormat=cobertura are used when running Coverlet with .NET test commands (e.g., *dotnet test*) to enable code coverage collection and specify the output format. This is the default configuration given by the Coverlet documentation for Azure DevOps; I just had to set up my project relative path. However, unlike the Microsoft.NET.Test.Sdk, we have here to create the publish coverage task. I'll give you the Coverlet documentation at the end of the section where you can learn more about it.

The YAML file is now ready, and if we push the code in the Git repository, as you may know, it will trigger the pipeline, and it should give the following result (on the same Code Coverage panel) as shown in Figure 5-24.

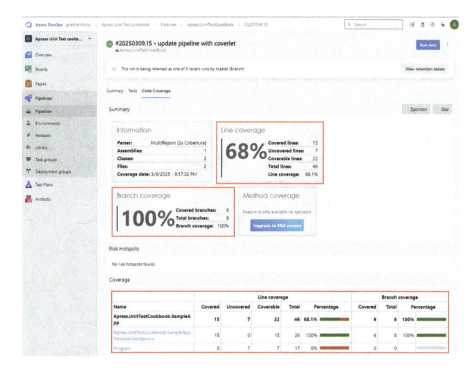

Figure 5-24. *The code coverage report in Azure DevOps with Coverlet*

As you can see the report is more detailed; we can even check the coverage per class and per assembly.

If you want to run it in a command prompt, you'll have to use the following command:

```
dotnet test /p:CollectCoverage=true /p:CoverletOutputFormat
=cobertura
```

The output is shown in Figure 5-25.

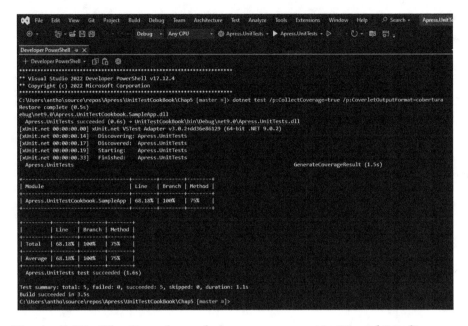

Figure 5-25. *The Coverlet code coverage report in Visual Studio*

Personally, I love the output format in the command prompt! And you? 😊

You may also have noticed that the *Program* class is back. It's normal since Coverlet needs its own settings; the preceding *coverage.runsettings* won't work with Coverlet because it simply does not support external files as code coverage configurations. There are three main ways to exclude some code:

1. The ExcludeFromCodeCoverage attribute

2. Editing the test project's csproj file

3. Writing command line arguments

You already know the *ExcludeFromCodeCoverage* attribute, so I'll show you how to edit the csproj file and how to write command line arguments.

Excluding Code by Editing the csproj File of Your Test Project

The template for excluding code in the csproj file looks like Listing 5-7.

Listing 5-7. The csproj template section for code coverage exclusion

```
<PropertyGroup>
  <CollectCoverage>true</CollectCoverage>
  <CoverletOutputFormat>cobertura</CoverletOutputFormat>

  <!-- Exclude specific assemblies -->
  <Exclude>[MyNamespace.*]*</Exclude>

  <!-- Exclude specific files -->
  <ExcludeByFile>**/GeneratedCode/*.cs</ExcludeByFile>

  <!-- Exclude specific attributes -->
  <ExcludeByAttribute>Obsolete,GeneratedCode</ExcludeBy
  Attribute>
</PropertyGroup>
```

We can exclude code from its namespace, from its filename, or by its attributes. The * (asterisk) is a wildcard for matching multiple elements. In our case, if we want to exclude the *Program.cs* file (the *Program* class), we have to edit the section as shown in Listing 5-8.

Listing 5-8. Excluding the Program class in the csproj file

```
<PropertyGroup>
  <CollectCoverage>true</CollectCoverage>
  <CoverletOutputFormat>cobertura</CoverletOutputFormat>
  <!-- Exclude specific files -->
  <ExcludeByFile>**/Program.cs</ExcludeByFile>
</PropertyGroup>
```

Excluding Code by Using Command Line Arguments

If we want to exclude the Program class by a command line argument, add the following argument (`/p:Exclude="[*]*Program*"`) in your commands as follows:

```
arguments: '--configuration $(buildConfiguration)
/p:CollectCoverage=true /p:CoverletOutputFormat=cobertura
/p:Exclude="[*]*Program*"' for the YAML pipeline
```

dotnet test `/p:CollectCoverage=true /p:CoverletOutputFormat=cobertura /p:Exclude="[*]*Program*"` for the test command in a command prompt

The `/p:Exclude` parameter in Coverlet allows you to specify patterns for excluding certain files, classes, or namespaces from code coverage analysis. The pattern `/p:Exclude="[*]*Program*"` applies this exclusion to all assemblies (*[*]*), filtering out any code element containing "Program" in its name. This is commonly used to exclude *Program.cs*, which typically contains startup logic rather than testable business code. By excluding such files, the coverage report focuses on meaningful application logic, providing a more accurate representation of test coverage.

If we execute the edited command in Azure DevOps, it should show a coverage of 100% as shown in Figure 5-26.

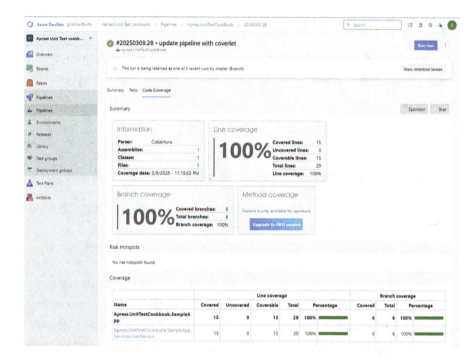

Figure 5-26. *The code coverage report in Azure DevOps with Coverlet and some code excluded*

Isn't great? 😊

I haven't been through all the capabilities of Coverlet in this section; I just wanted to introduce you to this tool, which is the best recommended for generating code coverage reports. If you want to learn more about it, you can read the Coverlet documentation on GitHub: `https://github.com/coverlet-coverage/coverlet/blob/master/Documentation/MSBuildIntegration.md`.

Summary

This chapter explored the automation of unit tests to improve development efficiency, reliability, and CI integration. It covered automating tests in Visual Studio using Live Unit Testing, which provides real-time feedback on test coverage. The chapter then explained Azure DevOps, focusing on Azure Repos and Azure Pipelines, to automate unit test execution through a YAML-based CI pipeline. It also detailed how to set up a Git repository, create a CI pipeline, and track pipeline execution results. Finally, it emphasized the importance of measuring code coverage in Visual Studio and Azure DevOps (with and without Coverlet) to ensure thorough testing and maintain high code quality. I hope you enjoyed it. The next chapter will discuss a unit testing case study. See you there!

CHAPTER 6

Case Study

As the final chapter of this book, I want to present a case study in unit testing. This chapter bridges theory and practice by demonstrating real-world testing applications through a simple example. It highlights common pitfalls such as poor architecture and coding practices while showcasing best practices for writing maintainable and effective tests. By comparing bad and good approaches, you'll observe progressive improvements and gain a deeper understanding of proper coding, architecture, and unit testing. To illustrate these concepts, I'll use a small ASP.NET Core Web API. In this chapter, I will show you

- What not to do

- How to refactor your application with the best practices

- How to unit test your application

What Not to Do

Unfortunately, when you start in software development or join an ongoing project, you will likely encounter a poorly coded and/or poorly architected application. As a result, maintainability becomes challenging, and testing the application becomes difficult, if not impossible.

Let's consider the following Web API, which includes two endpoints, *GetById* and *Create*, within a controller named *OrdersController*. The entire application is coded in a single file, including the Entity Framework Core

© Anthony Giretti 2025
A. Giretti, *The Unit Testing Practice Cookbook*,
https://doi.org/10.1007/979-8-8688-1454-9_6

entity definitions, the *DbContext*, and the *Order* model, which is used end to end from the database to the final endpoint. Last thing, some validation is performed on the *Order* class through the *ValidateOrder* private method. For readability, I have deliberately omitted the API configuration (*Program.cs*). Listing 6-1 shows the *OrdersController.cs* file.

Listing 6-1. The OrdersController file

```
using Microsoft.AspNetCore.Mvc;
using Microsoft.EntityFrameworkCore;
using System;
using System.Linq;
using System.Threading.Tasks;

namespace Apress.UnitTestCookbook.Controllers
{
    [ApiController]
    [Route("api/[controller]")]
    public class OrdersController : ControllerBase
    {
        private readonly AppDbContext _context;

        public OrdersController(AppDbContext context)
        // Directly dependent on DbContext
        {
            _context = context;
        }

        [HttpGet("{id}")]
        public async Task<IActionResult> GetById(int id)
        {
            var order = await _context.Orders.FindAsync(id);

            if (order == null)
```

```
    {
        return NotFound();
    }

    return Ok(order);
}

[HttpPost]
public async Task<IActionResult> Create([FromBody]
Order order)
{
    if (!ValidateOrder(order)) // Private validation method
    {
        return BadRequest("Invalid order details.");
    }

    _context.Orders.Add(order);
    await _context.SaveChangesAsync();

    return CreatedAtAction(nameof(GetOrder), new
    { id = order.Id }, order);
}

private bool ValidateOrder(Order order)
// Private validation logic (BAD)
{
    if (order == null || string.IsNullOrWhiteSpace
    (order.ProductName) || order.Price <= 0)
    {
        return false;
    }
    return true;
}
}
```

```
public class AppDbContext : DbContext
{
    public AppDbContext(DbContextOptions<AppDbContext>
    options) : base(options) { }
    public DbSet<Order> Orders { get; set; }
}

public class Order
{
    public int Id { get; set; }
    public string ProductName { get; set; }
    public decimal Price { get; set; }
}
}
```

What's wrong with this code? (And believe me it's happening very often.) There are four points here:

1. **Tightly Coupled**: The controller handles validation + database + API logic, violating the *Single Responsibility Principle (SRP)*.

2. **No Dependency Injection**: Unable to mock anything.

3. **Private Validation Method**: Cannot be unit tested separately.

4. **Hard to Extend**: If validation rules change, we must modify the controller.

You've got it! Before we can unit test our API, we first need to refactor it to make it testable. So let's get started!

Refactor Your Application with the Best Practices

Here's a breakdown of how we should **refactor the untestable** API **into a testable** API, with one bullet point per change:

1. **Created a Domain layer:** Moved any interface, enums, and domain object (*Order* class). To summarize any abstraction or domain object visible through the entire application.

2. **Extracted Validation Logic:** Moved validation from a private method inside *OrdersController* to an injectable *IOrderValidator* service defined in the Domain layer.

3. **Introduced Dependency Injection:** *OrdersController* now depends on *IOrderService* instead of directly using *DbContext*.

4. **Created a Service Layer (*OrderService* and *OrderValidator* Classes):** Encapsulated business logic, validation, and database interactions separately.

5. **Created a Repository Layer (*OrderRepository, OrderEntityMapper*):** Isolated data access from business logic, making *DbContext* an implementation detail, defining an *OrderEntity* class that relies only on the database even though its implementation is similar to the *Order* class, and mapping between *Order* and *OrderEntity* classes through the *OrderEntityMapper* static class.

6. **Used an Enum (*Statuses*)**: Improved readability by defining response statuses (Success, Invalid, NotFound), defined in the Domain layer.

7. **Changed Error Handling to List<string>**: Allowed multiple validation errors instead of a single message to return more accurate errors.

8. **Made OrderService Return Tuples**: Standardized method outputs with (status, result, errors), improving clarity where the result is the *Order* class.

9. **Refactored OrdersController**: Made it only responsible for handling HTTP requests and responses.

10. **Enabled Unit Testing via Interfaces and a Static Class**: *IOrderService*, *IOrderValidator*, and *IOrderRepository* interfaces are now mockable for tests. The *OrderEntityMapper* static class can be static since it is invoked within the *OrderRepository* class. The *OrderRepository* class won't be unit tested. It's an infrastructure component; there is no need to make the *OrderEntityMapper* class mockable.

The API project should look like Figure 6-1 in Visual Studio.

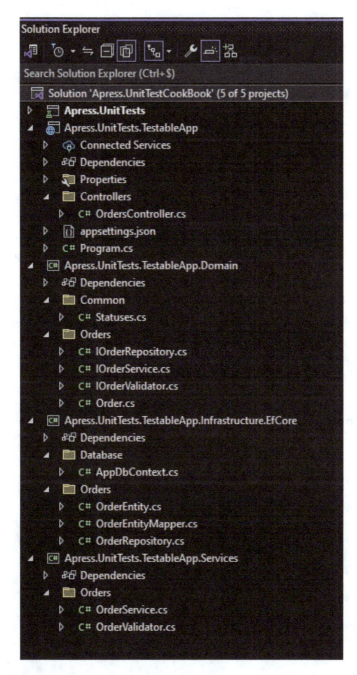

Figure 6-1. *The API project organization*

As you can see, the architecture is now cleaner with a clear *separation of concern (SoC)*. Here is a summary of the new architecture:

1. **API layer** (controllers in TestableApp)

2. **Domain layer** (interfaces and models in TestableApp.Domain)

3. **Infrastructure layer** (database, repositories, mappers in TestableApp.Infrastructure.EfCore)

4. **Service layer** (business logic in TestableApp. Services)

This architecture now enables testability. Let's go through these classes to see how they are structured. In the next section, I'll provide more details on unit test implementation. However, I won't dive into every class in detail to avoid overwhelming you with unnecessary explanations—our focus remains on unit testing. Each of the following files is referenced by its corresponding listing number:

OrdersController.cs: Listing 6-2

Statuses.cs: Listing 6-3

IOrderRepository.cs: Listing 6-4

IOrderService.cs: Listing 6-5

IOrderValidator.cs: Listing 6-6

Order.cs: Listing 6-7

AppDbContext.cs: Listing 6-8

OrderEntity.cs: Listing 6-9

OrderEntityMapper.cs: Listing 6-10

OrderRepository.cs: Listing 6-11

OrderService.cs: Listing 6-12

OrderValidator.cs: Listing 6-13

Let's now take a look at the implementation of each of these files. I will go into detail for the classes that we will be testing in the next section.

Listing 6-2. The OrdersController.cs file

```
using Apress.UnitTests.TestableApp.Domain.Common;
using Apress.UnitTests.TestableApp.Domain.Orders;
using Microsoft.AspNetCore.Mvc;
using System.Diagnostics.CodeAnalysis;

namespace Apress.UnitTests.TestableApp.Controllers;

[Route("api/[controller]")]
[ApiController]
public class OrdersController : ControllerBase
{
    private readonly IOrderService _orderService;

    public OrdersController(IOrderService orderService)
    {
        _orderService = orderService;
    }

    [HttpGet("{id}")]
    public async Task<IActionResult> GetById(int id)
    {
        var (status, order, errors) = await _orderService.Get
        ByIdAsync(id);

        if (status == Statuses.NotFound)
            return NotFound(errors);
```

```
        return Ok(order);
    }

    [HttpPost]
    public async Task<IActionResult> Create([FromBody]
    Order order)
    {
        var (status, id, errors) = await _orderService.Create
        Async(order);

        if (status == Statuses.Invalid)
            return BadRequest(errors);

        if (id <= 0)
            return UnprocessableEntity();

        return CreatedAtAction(nameof(Create), new { id
}, null);
    }
}
```

Listing 6-3. The Statuses.cs file

```
namespace Apress.UnitTests.TestableApp.Domain.Common;

public enum Statuses
{
    Success,
    NotFound,
    Invalid
}
```

Listing 6-4. The IOrderRepository.cs file

```
namespace Apress.UnitTests.TestableApp.Domain.Orders;

public interface IOrderRepository
{
    Task<Order> GetByIdAsync(int id);
    Task<int> AddAsync(Order order);
}
```

Listing 6-5. The IOrderService.cs file

```
using Apress.UnitTests.TestableApp.Domain.Common;

namespace Apress.UnitTests.TestableApp.Domain.Orders;

public interface IOrderService
{
    Task<(Statuses, Order, List<string>)> GetByIdAsync(int id);
    Task<(Statuses, int?, List<string>)>
CreateAsync(Order order);
}
```

Listing 6-6. The IOrderValidator.cs file

```
namespace Apress.UnitTests.TestableApp.Domain.Orders;

public interface IOrderValidator
{
    List<string> Validate(Order order);
}
```

Listing 6-7. The Order.cs file

```
namespace Apress.UnitTests.TestableApp.Domain.Orders;

public class Order
{
    public int Id { get; set; }
    public string ProductName { get; set; }
    public decimal Price { get; set; }
}
```

Listing 6-8. The AppDbContext.cs file

```
using Apress.UnitTests.TestableApp.Infrastructure.
EfCore.Orders;
using Microsoft.EntityFrameworkCore;
using System.Diagnostics.CodeAnalysis;

namespace Apress.UnitTests.TestableApp.Infrastructure.EfCore.
Database;

[ExcludeFromCodeCoverage]
public class AppDbContext : DbContext
{
    public AppDbContext(DbContextOptions<AppDbContext> options)
: base(options) { }
    public DbSet<OrderEntity> Orders { get; set; }
}
```

Listing 6-9. The OrderEntity.cs file

```
using System.Diagnostics.CodeAnalysis;

namespace Apress.UnitTests.TestableApp.Infrastructure.
EfCore.Orders;

public class OrderEntity
{
    public int Id { get; set; }
    public string ProductName { get; set; }
    public decimal Price { get; set; }
}
```

Listing 6-10. The OrderEntityMapper.cs file

```
using Apress.UnitTests.TestableApp.Domain.Orders;

namespace Apress.UnitTests.TestableApp.Infrastructure.
EfCore.Orders;

public static class OrderEntityMapper
{
    public static OrderEntity ToEntity(this Order order)
    {
        if (order is null)
            return null;

        return new()
        {
            Id = order.Id,
            ProductName = order.ProductName,
            Price = order.Price,
        };
    }
```

```
    public static Order FromEntity(this OrderEntity orderEntity)
    {
        if (orderEntity is null)
            return null;

        return new()
        {
            Id = orderEntity.Id,
            ProductName = orderEntity.ProductName,
            Price = orderEntity.Price,
        };
    }
}
```

Listing 6-11. The OrderRepository.cs file

```
using Apress.UnitTests.TestableApp.Domain.Orders;
using Apress.UnitTests.TestableApp.Infrastructure.EfCore.
Database;
using Microsoft.EntityFrameworkCore;
using System.Diagnostics.CodeAnalysis;
namespace Apress.UnitTests.TestableApp.Infrastructure.
EfCore.Orders;

[ExcludeFromCodeCoverage]
public class OrderRepository : IOrderRepository
{
    private readonly AppDbContext _context;

    public OrderRepository(AppDbContext context)
    {
        _context = context;
    }
```

```
public async Task<Order> GetByIdAsync(int id)
{
    return (await _context.Orders.Where(x => x.Id == id).
    SingleAsync()).FromEntity();
}

public async Task<int> AddAsync(Order order)
{
    var entity = order.ToEntity();
    if (entity is null)
        return 0;

    _context.Orders.Add(entity);
    return await _context.SaveChangesAsync();
}
}
```

Listing 6-12. The OrderService.cs file

```
using Apress.UnitTests.TestableApp.Domain.Common;
using Apress.UnitTests.TestableApp.Domain.Orders;

namespace Apress.UnitTests.TestableApp.Services.Orders;

public class OrderService : IOrderService
{
    private readonly IOrderRepository _orderRepository;
    private readonly IOrderValidator _orderValidator;

    public OrderService(IOrderRepository orderRepository,
    IOrderValidator orderValidator)
    {
        _orderRepository = orderRepository;
        _orderValidator = orderValidator;
    }
```

```
    public async Task<(Statuses, Order, List<string>)> GetBy
    IdAsync(int id)
    {
        var order = await _orderRepository.GetByIdAsync(id);

        if (order == null)
            return (Statuses.NotFound, null, new List<string> {
            "Order not found." });

        return (Statuses.Success, order, new List<string>());
    }

    public async Task<(Statuses, int?, List<string>)>
    CreateAsync(Order order)
    {
        var validationErrors = _orderValidator.Validate(order);
        if (validationErrors.Count > 0)
            return (Statuses.Invalid, null, validationErrors);

        var id = await _orderRepository.AddAsync(order);

        return (Statuses.Success, id, new List<string>());
    }
}
```

Listing 6-13. The OrderValidator.cs file

```
using Apress.UnitTests.TestableApp.Domain.Orders;

namespace Apress.UnitTests.TestableApp.Services.Orders;

public class OrderValidator : IOrderValidator
{
    public List<string> Validate(Order order)
    {
        var errors = new List<string>();
```

```
if (order == null)
{
    errors.Add("Order cannot be null.");
    return errors;
}
if (string.IsNullOrWhiteSpace(order.ProductName))
{
    errors.Add("Product name is required.");
}
if (order.Price <= 0)
{
    errors.Add("Price must be greater than zero.");
}

    return errors;
    }
}
```

These changes made the API (except the infrastructure code such as controllers, *Program.cs*, and the repositories) testable and maintainable. In the next section I'll show you the unit tests of the *OrderService*, *OrderValidator*, and *OrderEntityMapper* classes where the critical business logic takes place.

Unit Test Your Application

To continue what we covered together throughout this book, we will now move on to more practice by using the libraries NSubstitute, AutoFixture, FluentAssertions, and ExpectedObjects, along with xUnit for our unit tests. Here, we will test all possible scenarios that the *OrderService*, *OrderValidator*, and *OrderEntityMapper* classes implement.

For the unit tests themselves, I have created a specific file structure. What I like to do, and what I consider a **good practice**, is to structure the unit test project folders by responsibility, with one folder per tested project. Inside each project folder, I create a separate folder for each tested class, and within each class-specific folder, I create one test file per tested method. This approach enhances readability and maintainability. Figure 6-2 shows the test project folder structure, including tests for the *OrderService*, *OrderValidator*, and *OrderEntityMapper* classes.

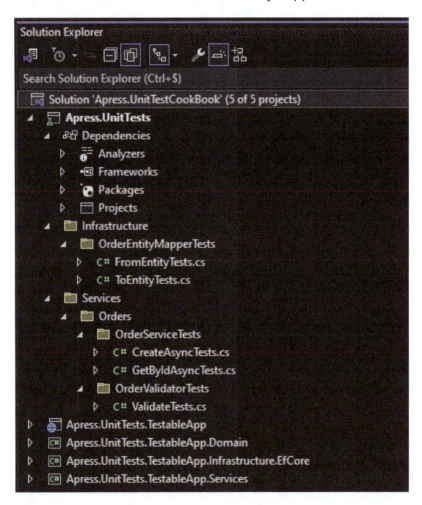

Figure 6-2. *The unit test project organization*

Now, let's go through each unit test one by one.

Unit Testing the OrderService Class

Key Components and Responsibilities

The *OrderService* class is responsible for handling business logic related to orders. It interacts with both the data layer *(IOrderRepository)* and the validation layer *(IOrderValidator)*. The bullet list below explains what the *OrderService* class does exactly in order to better understand how to unit test it:

1. **Implements *IOrderService***

    - This ensures the class follows an interface-driven design, making it easier to mock in tests.

2. **Dependencies via Dependency Injection**

    - Uses *IOrderRepository* for database operations.

    - Uses *IOrderValidator* to ensure the validity of *Order* objects.

3. **Method**: *GetByIdAsync(int id)*

    - Calls *_orderRepository.GetByIdAsync(id)* to retrieve an order from the database.

    - If no order is found, returns a tuple with

        - *Statuses.NotFound*

        - null (since no order exists)

        - A list containing the error message "Order not found."

- If the order is found, returns

  - *Statuses.Success*

  - The found *Order* object

  - An empty list (no errors)

4. **Method**: *CreateAsync(Order order)*

- Calls *_orderValidator.Validate(order)* to validate the order before saving.

- If validation fails, returns

  - *Statuses.Invalid*

  - null (no id assigned)

  - A list of validation errors

- If validation passes, it adds the order to the repository (*_orderRepository.AddAsync(order)*) and returns

  - *Statuses.Success*

  - The newly created order id

  - An empty list (no errors)

The Unit Tests

We have two methods to test: *CreateAsync* and *GetByIdAsync*. So I created two test files. Let's start with the tests for the *GetByIdAsync* method.

Testing the GetByIdAsync Method

Listing 6-14 presents the *GetByIdAsyncTests* class, which includes two tests that comprehensively cover all possible scenarios of the *GetByIdAsync* method's behavior.

Listing 6-14. The GetByIdAsyncTests class

```
using Apress.UnitTests.TestableApp.Domain.Common;
using Apress.UnitTests.TestableApp.Domain.Orders;
using Apress.UnitTests.TestableApp.Services.Orders;
using AutoFixture;
using FluentAssertions;
using NSubstitute;
using Xunit;

namespace Apress.UnitTests.Services.Orders.OrderServiceTests;

public class GetByIdAsyncTests
{
    private readonly IOrderRepository _orderRepository;
    private readonly IOrderValidator _orderValidator;
    private readonly IOrderService _orderService;
    private readonly Fixture _fixture;

    public GetByIdAsyncTests()
    {
        _orderRepository = Substitute.For<IOrderRepository>();
        _orderValidator = Substitute.For<IOrderValidator>();
        _orderService = new OrderService(_orderRepository,
        _orderValidator);
        _fixture = new Fixture();
    }
```

```
[Fact]
public async Task GetByIdAsync_WhenGetOrderByIdAsync
ReturnsNull_ShouldReturnNotFoundAndNullOrderAndASingle
SpecificError()
{
    // Arrange
    var orderId = _fixture.Create<int>();
    _orderRepository.GetByIdAsync(Arg.Any<int>())
    .Returns((Order)null);

    // Act
    var (status, order, errors) = await _orderService
    .GetByIdAsync(orderId);

    // Assert
    status.Should().Be(Statuses.NotFound);
    order.Should().BeNull();
    errors.Should().ContainSingle("Order not found.");
    await _orderRepository.Received(1).GetByIdAsync
    (Arg.Is(orderId));
}

[Fact]
public async Task GetByIdAsync_WhenGetOrderByIdAsync
ReturnsAnOrder_ShouldReturnSuccessAndOrderAndWithAnyError()
{
    // Arrange
    var order = _fixture.Create<Order>();
    _orderRepository.GetByIdAsync(order.Id).Returns(order);

    // Act
    var (status, resultOrder, errors) = await _order
    Service.GetByIdAsync(order.Id);
```

```
    // Assert
    status.Should().Be(Statuses.Success);
    resultOrder.Should().Be(order);
    errors.Should().BeEmpty();
    await _orderRepository.Received(1).GetByIdAsync
    (Arg.Is(order.Id));
  }
}
```

Explanations are as follows.

The GetByIdAsync_WhenGetOrderByIdAsyncReturnsNull_Should ReturnNotFoundAndNullOrderAndASingleSpecificError Test Method

The test verifies that when _orderRepository.GetByIdAsync() returns null, the method correctly returns *Statuses.NotFound*, a null order, and a single error message: "Order not found." Additionally, it ensures that _orderRepository.GetByIdAsync(id) is called exactly once.

The GetByIdAsync_WhenGetOrderByIdAsyncReturnsAnOrder_Should ReturnSuccessAndOrderAndWithAnyError Test Method

The test confirms that when _orderRepository.GetByIdAsync() returns a valid *Order*, the method correctly returns *Statuses.Success*, the expected *Order* object, and an empty error list. It also ensures that _orderRepository. GetByIdAsync(id) is called exactly once.

Testing the CreateAsync Method

Listing 6-15 presents the *CreateAsyncTests* class, which includes two tests that comprehensively cover all possible scenarios of the *CreateAsync* method's behavior.

Listing 6-15. The CreateAsyncTests class

```
using Apress.UnitTests.TestableApp.Domain.Common;
using Apress.UnitTests.TestableApp.Domain.Orders;
using Apress.UnitTests.TestableApp.Services.Orders;
using AutoFixture;
using FluentAssertions;
using NSubstitute;
using Xunit;

namespace Apress.UnitTests.Services.Orders.OrderServiceTests;

public class CreateAsyncTests
{
    private readonly IOrderRepository _orderRepository;
    private readonly IOrderValidator _orderValidator;
    private readonly IOrderService _orderService;
    private readonly Fixture _fixture;

    public CreateAsyncTests()
    {
        _orderRepository = Substitute.For<IOrderRepository>();
        _orderValidator = Substitute.For<IOrderValidator>();
        _orderService = new OrderService(_orderRepository,
        _orderValidator);
        _fixture = new Fixture();
    }

    [Fact]
    public async Task CreateAsync_WhenValidationReturnsAn
    Error_ShouldReturnInvalidAndIdNullAndProperError()
    {
        // Arrange
        var order = _fixture.Create<Order>();
```

```
_orderValidator.Validate(order).Returns(new List<string>
{ "A single error." });

// Act
var (status, id, errors) = await _orderService.
CreateAsync(order);

// Assert
status.Should().Be(Statuses.Invalid);
id.Should().BeNull();
errors.Should().ContainSingle("Invalid data.");
_orderValidator.Received(1).Validate(Arg.Is(order));
await _orderRepository.DidNotReceive().AddAsync
(Arg.Any<Order>());
}

[Fact]
public async Task CreateAsync_WhenValidationReturns
SeveralErrors_ShouldReturnInvalidAndIdNullAndAllProper
Errors()
{
    // Arrange
    var order = _fixture.Create<Order>();
    _orderValidator.Validate(order).Returns(new List<string>
    { "Error1.", "Error2." });

    // Act
    var (status, id, errors) = await _orderService.CreateAsync
    (order);

    // Assert
    status.Should().Be(Statuses.Invalid);
    id.Should().BeNull();
    errors.Should()
```

```
            .HaveCount(2)
            .And
            .Contain("Error1.")
            .And.
            Contain("Error2.");
        _orderValidator.Received(1).Validate(Arg.Is(order));
        await _orderRepository.DidNotReceive().AddAsync
        (Arg.Any<Order>());
    }

    [Fact]
    public async Task CreateAsync_WhenValidationReturnsNo
    Error_ShouldReturnIdNotNullAndSuccessAndEmptyError()
    {
        // Arrange
        var order = _fixture.Create<Order>();
        var orderId = _fixture.Create<int>();
        _orderValidator.Validate(order).Returns(new
        List<string>());
        _orderRepository.AddAsync(order).Returns(orderId);

        // Act
        var (status, id, errors) = await _orderService.Create
        Async(order);

        // Assert
        status.Should().Be(Statuses.Success);
        id.Should().Be(orderId);
        _orderValidator.Received(1).Validate(Arg.Is(order));
        await _orderRepository.Received(1).AddAsync
        (Arg.Is(order));
    }
}
```

Explanations are as follows.

The CreateAsync_WhenValidationReturnsAnError_ ShouldReturnInvalidAndIdNullAndProperError Test Method

This test verifies that when the order validation fails with a single error, *CreateAsync* returns *Statuses.Invalid*, a null id, and the expected error message. It ensures that *_orderValidator.Validate(order)* is called once and that *_orderRepository.AddAsync(order)* is never called (since an invalid order should not be saved).

The CreateAsync_WhenValidationReturnsSeveralErrors_ ShouldReturnInvalidAndIdNullAndAllProperErrors Test Method

This test checks that when multiple validation errors occur, *CreateAsync* returns *Statuses.Invalid*, a null id, and a list containing all expected error messages. It ensures *_orderValidator.Validate(order)* is called exactly once and *_orderRepository.AddAsync(order)* is never executed.

The CreateAsync_WhenValidationReturnsNoError_ ShouldReturnIdNotNullAndSuccessAndEmptyError Test Method

This test ensures that when validation passes with no errors, *CreateAsync* returns *Statuses.Success*, a non-null order id, and an empty error list. It verifies that *_orderValidator.Validate(order)* is called once, and *_orderRepository.AddAsync(order)* is successfully executed exactly once with the correct order.

Unit Testing the OrderValidator Class

Key Components and Responsibilities

The *OrderValidator* class is responsible for validating *Order* objects before they are processed by the system. It ensures that orders meet the required

187

business rules and constraints. The bullet list below explains what the *OrderValidator* class does exactly in order to better understand how to unit test it:

1. Implements *IOrderValidator*

2. **Method**: *Validate(Order order)*

    - Checks if the order is null

        - If the order is null, returns a list containing "Order cannot be null."

    - Validates the product name

        - Ensures the *ProductName* property is not null, empty, or whitespace.

        - If invalid, adds "Product name is required." to the error list.

    - Validates the price

        - Ensures the *Price* property is greater than 0.

        - If invalid, adds "Price must be greater than zero." to the error list.

    - Returns a list of errors

        - If the order is valid, returns an **empty list** (no errors).

        - If validation fails, returns a **list containing all detected errors**.

The Unit Tests

We have a single method to test: *Validate*. Then I created a single test file named *ValidateTests.cs*.

Testing the Validate Method

Listing 6-16 presents the *ValidateTests* class, which includes five tests that comprehensively cover all possible scenarios of the *Validate* method's behavior.

Listing 6-16. The ValidateTests class

```
using Apress.UnitTests.TestableApp.Domain.Orders;
using Apress.UnitTests.TestableApp.Services.Orders;
using AutoFixture;
using FluentAssertions;
using Xunit;

namespace Apress.UnitTests.Services.Orders.OrderValidatorTests;

public class ValidateTests
{
    private readonly OrderValidator _validator;
    private readonly Fixture _fixture;

    public ValidateTests()
    {
        _validator = new OrderValidator();
        _fixture = new Fixture();
    }

    [Fact]
    public void Validate_WhenOrderisNull_ShouldReturnSingle
    ErrorOrderCannotBeNull()
```

```
    {
        // Arrange
        var order = (Order)null;

        // Act
        var errors = _validator.Validate(order);

        // Assert
        errors.Should().ContainSingle("Order cannot be null.");
    }

    [Theory]
    [InlineData("")]
    [InlineData(" ")]
    [InlineData(null)]
    public void Validate_WhenOrderIsNotNullAndProductName
    IsNullOrEmpty_ShouldReturnASingleSpecificError(string
    productName)
    {
        // Arrange
        var order = _fixture.Build<Order>()
                            .With(o => o.ProductName, product
                            Name)
                            .Create();

        // Act
        var errors = _validator.Validate(order);

        // Assert
        errors.Should().ContainSingle("Product name is required.");
    }

    [Theory]
    [InlineData(0)]
```

```
[InlineData(-1)]
public void Validate_WhenOrderIsNotNullAndPriceEqualsZeroOr
Negative_ShouldReturnASingleSpecificError(decimal price)
{
    // Arrange
    var order = _fixture.Build<Order>()
                        .With(o => o.Price, price)
                        .Create();

    // Act
    var errors = _validator.Validate(order);

    // Assert
    errors.Should().ContainSingle("Price must be greater
    than zero.");
}

[Theory]
[InlineData("", 0)]
[InlineData(" ", 0)]
[InlineData(null, 0)]
[InlineData("", -1)]
[InlineData(" ", -1)]
[InlineData(null, -1)]
public void Validate_WhenOrderIsNotNullAndPriceEquals
ZeroOrNegativeAndProductNameIsNullOrEmpty_ShouldReturnTwo
SpecificErrors(string productName, decimal price)
{
    // Arrange
    var order = _fixture.Build<Order>()
                        .With(o => o.Price, price)
                        .With(o => o.ProductName,
                        productName)
                        .Create();
```

```
    // Act
    var errors = _validator.Validate(order);

    // Assert
    errors.Should()
            .HaveCount(2)
            .And
            .Contain("Price must be greater than zero.")
            .And
            .Contain("Product name is required.");
    }

    [Fact]
    public void Validate_WhenOrderIsNotNullAndCorrectly
    Filled_ShouldReturnEmptyErrorList()
    {
        // Arrange
        var order = _fixture.Create<Order>();

        // Act
        var errors = _validator.Validate(order);

        // Assert
        errors.Should().BeEmpty();
    }
}
```

Explanations are as follows.

The Validate_WhenOrderisNull_ ShouldReturnSingleErrorOrderCannotBeNull Test Method

This test ensures that when a null order is passed to the validator, it returns a list containing only one error message: "Order cannot be null."

The Validate_WhenOrderIsNotNullAndProductNameIsNullOr Empty_ShouldReturnASingleSpecificError Test Method

This test uses parameterized testing with *Theory* and *InlineData* attributes to evaluate multiple cases where the *ProductName* property is empty, whitespace, or null. It verifies that in each of these scenarios, the validation consistently returns a single error message: "Product name is required."

The Validate_WhenOrderIsNotNullAndPriceEqualsZeroOr Negative_ShouldReturnASingleSpecificError Test Method

This test also employs parameterized testing to verify cases where the *Price* property is either 0 or negative. It ensures that the validator correctly returns a single error message "Price must be greater than zero." in these scenarios.

The Validate_WhenOrderIsNotNullAndPriceEqualsZeroOrNegative AndProductNameIsNullOrEmpty_ShouldReturnTwoSpecificErrors Test Method

This test evaluates scenarios where both the *ProductName* property is null or empty and the *Price* property is zero or negative. It ensures that the validation correctly returns both error messages in the list: "Product name is required." and "Price must be greater than zero."

The Validate_WhenOrderIsNotNullAndCorrectlyFilled_ShouldReturn EmptyErrorList Test Method

This test ensures that the validation returns an empty error list when an *Order* object is valid, meaning no validation errors occurred.

Unit Testing the OrderEntityMapper Class

Key Components and Responsibilities

The *OrderEntityMapper* class provides extension methods to convert between *Order* (domain model) and *OrderEntity* (database entity). The bullet list below explains what the *OrderEntityMapper* class does exactly in order to better understand how to unit test it:

1. **Static Utility Class**: Provides extension methods for mapping between Order and OrderEntity objects

2. **Method *ToEntity(Order order)*:** Converts a domain-level *Order* object into an *OrderEntity* for persistence in the database

3. **Method *FromEntity(OrderEntity orderEntity)*:** Converts an *OrderEntity* from the database back into an *Order* domain object

The Unit Tests

For this case, we have two methods to test: *ToEntity and FromEntity*. Then I created two test files named *FromEntityTests.cs* and *ToEntityTests.cs*.

Testing the ToEntity Method

Listing 6-17 presents the *ToEntityTests* class, which includes five tests that comprehensively cover all possible scenarios of the *ToEntity* method's behavior.

Listing 6-17. The ToEntityTests class

```
using Apress.UnitTests.TestableApp.Domain.Orders;
using Apress.UnitTests.TestableApp.Infrastructure.
EfCore.Orders;
using AutoFixture;
using ExpectedObjects;
using FluentAssertions;
using Xunit;

namespace Apress.UnitTests.Infrastructure.
OrderEntityMapperTests;

public class ToEntityTests
{
    private readonly Fixture _fixture;

    public ToEntityTests()
    {
        _fixture = new Fixture();
    }

    [Fact]
    public void ToEntity_WhenOrderIsNull_ShouldReturnNull()
    {
        // Arrange
        var order = (Order)null;

        // Act
        var result = order.ToEntity();

        // Assert
        result.Should().BeNull();
    }
```

```
[Fact]
public void ToEntity_WhenOrderIsNotNull_ShouldReturn
OrderEntityCorrectlyFilled()
{
    // Arrange
    var order = _fixture.Create<Order>();

    // Act
    var result = order.ToEntity();

    // Assert
    result.ToExpectedObject().ShouldEqual(new OrderEntity
    {
        Id = order.Id,
        ProductName = order.ProductName,
        Price = order.Price
    });
}
}
```

Explanations are as follows.

The ToEntity_WhenOrderIsNull_ShouldReturnNull Test Method

This test verifies that when a null *Order* object is passed to the *ToEntity* method, it correctly returns null, preventing null reference errors.

The ToEntity_WhenOrderIsNotNull_ShouldReturnOrder EntityCorrectlyFilled Method

This test verifies that when a valid *Order* object is converted using *ToEntity*, the resulting *OrderEntity* retains the same values as the original *Order*. It uses *ExpectedObjects* to ensure that all properties, including *Id*, *ProductName*, and *Price*, are correctly mapped.

Testing the FromEntity Method

Listing 6-18 presents the *FromEntityTests* class, which includes five tests that comprehensively cover all possible scenarios of the *FromEntity* method's behavior.

Listing 6-18. The FromEntityTests class

```
using Apress.UnitTests.TestableApp.Domain.Orders;
using Apress.UnitTests.TestableApp.Infrastructure.
EfCore.Orders;
using AutoFixture;
using ExpectedObjects;
using FluentAssertions;
using Xunit;

namespace Apress.UnitTests.Infrastructure.
OrderEntityMapperTests;

public class FromEntityTests
{
    private readonly Fixture _fixture;

    public FromEntityTests()
    {
        _fixture = new Fixture();
    }

    [Fact]
    public void FromEntity_WhenOrderEntityIsNull_Should
    ReturnNullOrder()
    {
        // Arrange
        var orderEntity = (OrderEntity)null;
```

```
    // Act
    var result = orderEntity.FromEntity();

    // Assert
    result.Should().BeNull();
}

[Fact]
public void FromEntity_WhenOrderEntityIsNotNull_Should
ReturnOrderCorrectlyFilled()
{
    // Arrange
    var orderEntity = _fixture.Create<OrderEntity>();

    // Act
    var result = orderEntity.FromEntity();

    // Assert
    result.ToExpectedObject().ShouldEqual(new Order
    {
        Id = orderEntity.Id,
        ProductName = orderEntity.ProductName,
        Price = orderEntity.Price
    });
}
}
```

Explanations are as follows.

The FromEntity_WhenOrderIsNull_ShouldReturnNull Test Method

This test ensures that if null is passed to the *FromEntity* method, it correctly returns null, preventing null reference exceptions.

The FromEntity_WhenOrderIsNotNull_ShouldReturnOrderEntity CorrectlyFilled

This test ensures that when a valid *Order* is converted to an *OrderEntity*, all properties (*Id*, *ProductName*, and *Price*) are accurately mapped. It uses ExpectedObjects to verify that the expected and actual objects match.

Summary

This chapter demonstrated how to refactor an untestable API by applying best practices such as dependency injection, separation of concerns, and structured architecture. It covers unit testing with NSubstitute, AutoFixture, FluentAssertions, and ExpectedObjects and xUnit ensuring comprehensive test coverage for key components like *OrderService*, *OrderValidator*, and *OrderEntityMapper* classes. Additionally, it introduced a structured test organization to improve readability and maintainability, bridging theory and real-world practice in unit testing. This example is truly a real-world scenario but in a simplified model, of course. If you follow the unit testing practices I have shown you in this chapter and throughout this book, you will be able to test any .NET application!

Index

A, B

Application programming
    interface (API)
    AppDbContext.cs file, 172
    explanations, 168, 169
    IOrderRepository.cs file, 171
    IOrderService.cs file, 171
    IOrderValidator.cs file, 171
    Order.cs file, 172
    OrderEntity.cs file, 173
    OrderEntityMapper.cs file, 173
    OrderRepository.cs file, 174
    OrdersController.cs file,
        169, 170
    OrderService.cs file, 175
    OrderValidator.cs file, 176, 177
    project organization, 167, 168
    refracting application, 165, 166
    separation of concern
        (SoC), 168
    Statuses.cs file, 170
Arrange, Act, Assert (AAA)
    pattern, 9
    arrange phase, 9
    execution (act) phase, 9
    preparation phase, 9
    verification (assert), 10

Automate testing
    code coverage
        capabilities, 151
        command line argument,
            157, 158
        Coverlet configuration,
            153, 154
        csproj file, 156
        DevOps, 149–151
        implementation, 141
        NuGet package, 152
        output format, 154
        Visual Studio, 141–149
        YAML file, 152, 153
    DevOps, 125–140
    Visual Studio (VS), 119–125

C

Clean code and architecture, 12
    architecture
        approaches, 18
        business logic layer, 19
        domain layer, 18
        external data access, 17
        infrastructure layers, 19
        interactions, 19

© Anthony Giretti 2025
A. Giretti, *The Unit Testing Practice Cookbook*,
https://doi.org/10.1007/979-8-8688-1454-9

Clean code and architecture (*cont.*)
    IOrderRepository
      interface, 22
    libraries/frameworks, 17
    low/high-level modules, 20
    mocking technique, 21
    NSubstitute library, 24–27
    optional tools, 19
    OrderService class, 22, 23
    presentation layer, 18
    requirements, 17
    testability, 17
    user interface, 17
  KISS principle, 12, 13
  private methods, 15, 16
  SOLID principles, 14, 15
  YAGNI, 13, 14
Command line interface (CLI), 32
  cd (change directory)
    command, 72
  execution output, 74
  project dependencies, 73
  running process, 73
  terminal/command prompt, 72
Continuous integration and
    deployment (CI/CD), 5, 125
  azure-pipeline.yml file, 128, 129
  Git repository, 131–139
    build details page, 138, 139
    code source, 133, 134
    overview, 140
    pipeline button, 133
    prompt creation, 132
    selection, 134, 135

    source control, 131
    task execution, 139, 140
    YAML file, 135, 136, 138
  steps, 127
  YAML file, 128–130

D, E, F, G

Dependency inversion principle
    (DIP), 15
Development/operations
    (DevOps)
  artifacts, 126
  boards, 125
  CI pipeline, 127–140
  code coverage
    percentage, 150, 151
    YAML file, 149, 150
  features, 125
  steps, 126, 127
Don't Repeat Yourself (DRY), 12

H

Hypertext transfer protocol
    (HttpClients)
  approaches, 109
  IHttpClientFactory, 113–115
  TagsService class, 113
  testing process
    BlogService class, 110, 111
    BlogServiceTests class,
      111, 112
    content-type, 112

I, J

Interface segregation principle
(ISP), 15

K

Keep it simple, stupid
(KISS), 12, 13

L, M

Liskov substitution principle
(LSP), 14

N

.NET applications
  abstract classes/virtual methods
    approaches, 107
    concepts, 106
    Employee class, 107
    EmployeeTests class,
      108, 109
    mocking framework, 107
  DataTables, 76
    datatable.json file, 81, 82
    DecimalJsonConverter
     class, 80
    EmbeddedJsonFileHelper
     class, 82
    IOrderRepository
     interface, 77
    order class, 76, 80
    OrderService class, 77, 78

OrderServiceTests
  class, 83, 84
  source code, 78, 79
DateTimes
  DateUtilities class, 85
  dependency injection, 86
  ISystemClock, 87, 88
  TimeProvider, 87, 89
  unit test, 88–90
excessive mocking, 116
extension methods, 90
  UserExtensions class, 91
  UserService class, 91–94
  UserUtilityService class, 93
HTTP (*see* HttpClients)
infrastructure components,
  116, 117
internal classes and
  methods, 103
  InternalsVisibleTo
   attribute, 105
  StringHelpers class, 104
  StringHelpersTests class,
   105, 106
logging method (ILogger), 94
  AuthenticationService
   class, 95
  AuthenticationServiceTests
   class, 96
  FakeLogger class, 98
  Log() Method, 95
  NuGet package, 97
  properties, 99
  virtual methods, 94

.NET applications (*cont.*)
overview, 75
private methods
AutoFixture/
FluentAssertions/xUnit, 102
encapsulation, 99
readability and reusability, 99
User class, 100
UserTests class, 101

O, P, Q, R

Open/closed principle (OCP), 14

S

Single responsibility principle
(SRP), 14
SOLID principles, 14, 15
System under test (SUT), 6, 113
calculator class, 6
clean code and architecture, 23
definition, 4
dependencies, 8
general approach, 6
identification, 6–8
output integers, 8
parameters, 7, 8

T

Team Foundation Version Control
(TFVC), 125
Test-driven development (TDD), 3

Testing applications
acceptance, 2
development cycle, 1
end-to-end testing, 2
functional testing, 2
integration, 2
performance, 2
smoke testing, 3
types of, 1
unit testing (*see* Unit testing)
Theory attribute, 34
empty value, 37
InlineData attribute, 35
main methods/
description, 40, 42
myNumber class member, 39
non-empty value, 36
string.IsNullOrEmpty
method, 35
Tools (unit test)
advantages
fact attribute, 33, 34
features, 32
string.IsNullOrEmpty
method, 33
Theory attribute, 34–42
xUnit, 33
AutoFixture, 28, 31
Address class, 47, 48
AddressTests class, 48–50
DeleteByIdAsync
method, 60, 61
GetByIdAsync method, 58
GetById method, 54

GetUserByStatusAsync
method, 55
IUserRepository interface, 53
possibilities, 51
User class, 53
UserService class, 53
UserServiceTests class,
55–57, 60
csproj, 30
ExpectedObjects, 29, 32
ExpectedObjects/NSubstitute
Employee class, 64
EmployeeService
class, 62, 63
EmployeeServiceTests
class, 65–67
ExpectedObjects, 67, 68
ILogAccessService
interface, 64
mocking dependencies, 62
object comparisons, 61, 62
FluentAssertions, 29, 32
advantages, 42
methods/description, 45–47
Person class, 43
PersonTests test class, 44, 45
Microsoft.NET.Test.Sdk, 29
NSubstitute, 28, 31, 52
NuGet packages, 27
running process
terminal/command
prompt, 72–74
Visual Studio, 68–72
xUnit, 28

xUnit package, 31
xunit.runner.visualstudio, 30

U

Unit testing
AAA pattern, 9, 10
automate (*see* Automate testing)
characteristics, 4, 5
clean code and
architecture, 11–26
concepts, 161
identification, 6–8
.NET (*see* .NET applications)
OrderEntityMapper class
components, 194
entity method, 194–196
FromEntity method, 197–199
OrdersController file, 162–165
OrderService class
CreateAsync
method's, 183–187
data/validation layer, 179
GetByIdAsync
method's, 181–183
methods, 180
validation errors, 187
project organization, 178, 179
refracting application, 165–177
tools (*see* Tools (unit test))
validation process
components/
responsibilities, 187, 188
ValidateTests class, 189–194

V, W, X

Visual Studio (VS)
  action code, 124
  code coverage, 141
    analyze, 142, 143
    auto detect runsettings
      files, 142
    blocks/lines, 148
    coverage.runsettings file, 141
    file structure, 141
    formulas, 148
    Functions node, 145
    ModulePaths node, 145
    results, 144
    results window, 146, 147
    updated files, 144, 145
    user class, 146
  configuration, 123
  configuration window, 121
  exclusion files, 122
  features, 119
  key settings, 122
  live unit testing window, 120
  lutignore file, 123, 124
  MSBuild processes, 122
  repository root, 122
  test case/process, 122
  testing process, 68–72
    results, 71, 72
    run button, 70, 71
    Test Explorer
      window, 69, 70
  xUnit project creation, 30

Y, Z

You Aren't Gonna Need It
  (YAGNI), 13, 14

GPSR Compliance
The European Union's (EU) General Product Safety Regulation (GPSR) is a set of rules that requires consumer products to be safe and our obligations to ensure this.

If you have any concerns about our products, you can contact us on

ProductSafety@springernature.com

In case Publisher is established outside the EU, the EU authorized representative is:

Springer Nature Customer Service Center GmbH
Europaplatz 3
69115 Heidelberg, Germany